I0181291

What Do We Know
and
How Do We Know It?

What Do We Know
and
How Do We Know It?

Making Informed Decisions in a World of Vested Interests

Greg Moore

Prairie Papers, LLC Pueblo, Colorado

What Do We Know and How Do We Know It?

Prairie Papers LLC
PO Box 9257
Pueblo, Colorado 81008

ISBN 978-1-7343751-0-7

This does not constitute an official release of CIA information. All statements of fact, opinion, or analysis expressed are those of the author and do not reflect the official positions or views of the Central Intelligence Agency (CIA) or any other U.S. Government agency. Nothing in the contents should be construed as asserting or implying U.S. Government authentication of information or CIA endorsement of the author's views. This material has been reviewed solely for classification.

Photo credit: Le Panda/Shutterstock.com

A great many people think they are thinking when they are merely rearranging their prejudices.

— *Most often credited to William James, 19th Century Philosopher*

Contents

Introduction

What do we know and how do we know it? Two simple and very direct questions that we probably don't use enough.

Together they are fundamental to better decision making because they encourage us to more closely examine the basis for decision and opinion. Is this foundation based on fact and the best judgement of those skilled in the art, or is it just something we fabricated based on little real evidence because we want it to be so? Too often, the honest answer is the last one.

As individuals, we tend to focus on the information and values that we want to believe, that are consistent with our individual experiences, and that our social group accepts. We ignore or heavily discount evidence that is inconvenient or contrary to our beliefs, and eagerly embrace information that supports our preferences. We don't have to look very far to find evidence of this. Consider, for example, the wide range of "indisputable" facts and rationalizations we have all heard on issues as diverse as medical treatment, environmental stewardship, gun control, religion, finances, gambling, and, of course, politics.

Different opinions and the decisions they engender are a fact of life and probably one of the reasons we have survived and progressed as a species. But not all of them are equally valid or useful. A life dominated by bad decisions can be a wasted opportunity. If we care about the quality of our decisions, we need to get the facts right and draw conclusions as honestly and fairly as possible. Our decisions can be no better than the information and reasoning that they are based on.

This book discusses some of the major challenges to making better decisions today. Specifically:

- What forces are at work when we think or reason about an issue?
- How are we manipulated to believe and act in certain ways?
- How should we evaluate different sources of information?
- Why is science so controversial?
- How do numerical concepts help and harm reasoning?

If we better understand these issues, perhaps we can then do a better job of deciding what to accept and reject, how to use that information, and back up any important decisions with a firm foundation, rather than simply rearranging our prejudices.[1]

The first step is accepting that most of our thinking is unconscious.

Two Ways of Thinking

We are unaware of most of the thinking that we do. We quickly recognize someone's face. A person's name suddenly pops into our head. We react instantly to an immediate threat. We like or dislike someone without really knowing them. We effortlessly drive home from work along a deserted road. This type of thinking is always going on, and we really have no idea how the thoughts it produces got where they are. There is no audit path to follow from where our brain started to where the idea popped into our consciousness.

Psychologists often refer to these unconscious thought processes as System 1. It is the source of intuitions, impressions, and feelings, and for many of the situations we encounter, System 1 works fine. We would not have survived as a species if we had to deliberate on everything that occurs in our lives. The tiger would have gotten us long before we weighed all of the possible options.

While we rely very heavily on System 1, it can handle some things poorly, particularly as relates to critical thinking and other difficult tasks. For example, System 1 doesn't deal very well with conflicting or competing ideas, or uncertainty, or math and statistics. It is fine with the flimsiest of evidence, and easily succumbs to bias and prejudice. As Daniel Kahneman notes in *Thinking Fast and Slow*, System 1 also has the nasty habit of answering the wrong question. If someone asks us how happy we are in our lives, for example, System 1 will answer with how we happen to feel at the moment, with no consideration of the longer term.[2]

Our deliberative thinking, on the other hand, requires much more effort and is done consciously by a process called, not surprisingly, System 2. System 2 works as we learn something new such as how to drive a car or ride a bike, or when we multiply two 10-digit numbers together, or consider how to resolve a medical problem, or wrestle with our income tax.[3]

We can see how these systems work together with a very simple puzzle known as the Muller-Lyer Illusion. Figure 1 shows two lines bracketed by arrows. Which line is longer?

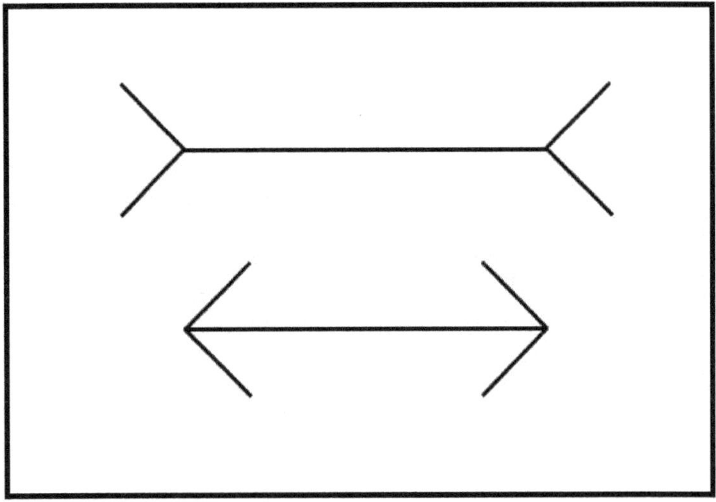

Figure 1. Muller-Lyer Illusion Which Line is Longer[4]

When this problem is encountered for the first time, most will see that the top line is longer than the bottom line. A ruler, however, will confirm that they are exactly the same length. Once a person has measured the lines, he or she will know this (the rationality of System 2 at work), but the two lines will still appear to be unequal (an effect of System 1). There is no way to stop System 1 from doing this. It is always on.

Are you more of a System 1 or System 2 problem solver? Are you more intuitive or more deliberative?

Here are three problems that will help to answer that question. What are the first answers that come to mind as you read them?

- A bat and ball cost $1.10. The bat costs one dollar more than the ball. How much does the ball cost?
- If it takes 5 machines 5 minutes to make 5 widgets, how long would it take 100 machines to make 100 widgets?
- In a lake, there is a patch of lily pads. Every day, the patch doubles in size. If it takes 48 days for the patch to cover the entire lake, how long would it take for the patch to cover half of the lake?

These three questions are designed to evoke an intuitive (System 1) answer that is wrong. If you quickly answered: $0.10, 100, and 24, and began to wonder why anyone would ask such easy questions, you might want to go back and engage System 2 a bit harder. On the other hand, if you perhaps thought $.10 for the first question, but immediately became suspicious, then your System 2 was working to correct a System 1 first impression. The correct answers are $0.05, 5 minutes, and 47 days.[5]

While we need both systems to survive in today's world, this book focuses mostly on critical thinking, or deliberation — the slow and careful consideration of an issue that is the domain of System 2.[6] If we are trying to decide how to stay healthy, whether or not to get that operation, for whom to vote, how to reach a fair compromise on a critical issue, what to invest in for the future, or trying to overcome biases that we are aware of, we need to closely examine outside information and temper whatever our intuition is telling us. In such circumstances, *what do we know and how do we know it?* really matters. We don't want to make such decisions solely on the basis of our gut feelings.

Synopsis

Much of the trouble we get into with decisions and beliefs is of our own doing. We can sometimes be sloppy thinkers, we often listen to the wrong thing, we almost never do the math, and we often do little to defend ourselves from those who would like to manipulate us. If we can better understand such poor habits and where the dangers to clear thinking lie, we can perhaps provide ourselves with a better frame of reference for thinking through problems and seeing other points of view.

The premise of this book is that we can create a more effective frame of reference for decision making through a better appreciation of our own rational weaknesses, a better understanding of how we can be deceived and manipulated by others, and by being more selective about our information sources. Since many of the problems that we face these days involve scientific findings, a more effective perspective should also include some appreciation of the strengths and limitations of science. And finally, numbers do matter in decisions, so an appreciation of basic quantitative tools can greatly strengthen one's frame of reference.

What Do We Know and How Do We Know It? addresses these issues in 6 primary chapters.

Chapter 1. We are Less Rational Than We Think. We often abuse logic, give common sense far too much credit, and are inherently a bit conspiratorial. In addition, we are often unable to recognize our own cognitive weaknesses. All of this makes us easy targets, and the first step is trying to see these weaknesses in better light.

Chapter 2. How the World Exploits Our Weaknesses. We live in a world full of deception, and often deliberately crafted by others who try to influence us. The better we understand how these deceptions are used, the easier it will be to meet the challenges that are thrown at us every day.

Chapter 3. Choosing Inputs Wisely. We get most of our information by some combination of reading, watching, thinking, talking, listening and doing. These create our experiences and provide the basis for what and how we believe. Consider, for example, how the individuals we hang out with in person or online influence us by what they do and what they say. Or how television influences our mannerisms and language and behavior. Or how a single negative encounter can change our life view. When issues really matter, like health and finances, for example, we should surround ourselves with the best decision-making capabilities that we can muster.

Chapter 4. Believing Science, but Not Scientists. Many of the challenges that we face today involve controversial science, such as the environment, nutrition, medical treatment, drug use, and education. But there is a difference between what science says and what a scientist at a university or an industrial laboratory writes in an article. This chapter explains why we should pay more attention to the former, and perhaps less to the latter.

Chapter 5. How Numbers Help and Harm Decisions. Ignoring tools such as high school algebra and statistics is like fighting with one hand tied behind our backs. If we don't know, for example, that 50% off the regular price and 50% more for the same price are not the same thing, or that there is more than one type of average, or that plummeting line on a graph might not mean what it seems, we are — as the old saying goes — ripe for the picking. This chapter will show how a few numbers and calculations can make a world of difference.

Chapter 6. Some Thoughts for the Future. Our future decision making will continue to become more entwined with technology, particularly as large data sets and AI become more prevalent in our lives. While it is not clear what forms future decision making will take, some will inevitably cede more decision-making to machines and others will involve more human-machine interactions (Alexa on steroids?). In any case, decisions will be made, and some will be better than others, depending on how well we understand what we know and how we know it. This chapter summarizes some of the more important strategies that should serve us well in future.

Expectations

The goal of this book is to help readers become less susceptible to believing anything that they just prefer to believe. The more gullible we are, the more we will suffer the consequences, whether they are simply the appearance of ignorance when we are with others, or negative effects of actions taken on the basis of misguided beliefs.

This is not a book about winning arguments with others, but rather about winning arguments with ourselves. For the purposes of this book, it does not matter where you or I sit on any particular issue. My intent is simply to help us all take a closer look at how we got where we are on issues.

For example, are we basing decisions on what we really know or on ideas and facts that we are simply echoing? Are the values we hold really ours, or those of someone who pushed us in one direction or another? Can we see and appreciate arguments from all sides of an issue? Have we cherry picked our way into a solution that is flawed? Can we keep our ego out of a decision? Do we listen, or do we just preach? Can we change our minds in light of compelling evidence? Is improvement something we believe that other people need more than us?

There is an old saying in the West that we don't try to make a horse drink, instead we salt his oats to make him want to drink. Some folks try to force facts down others' throats as if that will magically change their minds, but in general, this just annoys them. I am hopeful that this book will be a bit like salty oats and inspire curiosity, make us want to question our thoughts and those of others, and in general clean up our decision-making. The best lessons are those we figure out for ourselves.

Throughout this reading, please keep in mind that critical thinking is not about always being right the first time. Most people react badly when they discover they are wrong about something that they once believed. But we should dismiss those negative feelings and reactions. Understanding is a process of continuing improvement, and finding out that we are wrong can be a good outcome. As one of my colleagues often reminds me: all facts are friendly; what we do with them is what matters most.

CHAPTER ONE

We Are Less Rational Than We Think

The greatest deception that men suffer from is their own opinions — Leonardo Da Vinci

We've all experienced conversations in which we begin to think that the person doing the talking must be from another planet. But just because the speaker seems to be a bit delusional doesn't mean that we aren't too. This chapter will help us to become more aware of some of the flaws in our own thinking.[7]

We See Things That Aren't and Miss Things That Are

To begin with, we are not always aware of what is in front of us, even though we think we are. Some of this error is due to limitations in our ability to see and hear. Our eyes cannot see the ultraviolet portion of the electromagnetic spectrum that birds see and human ears cannot hear ultrasonic sounds that dogs hear. Bandwidth limitations like these are characteristic of all sensors. The cameras in our iPhones make great images in the visible part of the electromagnetic spectrum, for example, but they can't image the thermal radiation that is also in the scene being photographed.

In addition to fundamental restrictions in our sensors, limits also lie within the brain and how it processes the raw information that our sensors provide. As a result, what we *consciously* sense is not necessarily the same as the information that the sensors provide.

Scientists have developed a few tricks to help make some of these limits more obvious to us. For example, we have a blind spot in each of our retinas that lies at the point where the optic nerve is attached. There are no photoreceptors in that portion of the retina, but our brain conveniently fills in the blanks. Don't believe it? Take a look at Figure 2. Hold the page about a foot from your eyes and move it slowly toward your face. Keep your right eye closed and focus on the right-hand dot with your left eye. At some distance, you will no longer be able to see the left-hand dot. There's your blind spot.

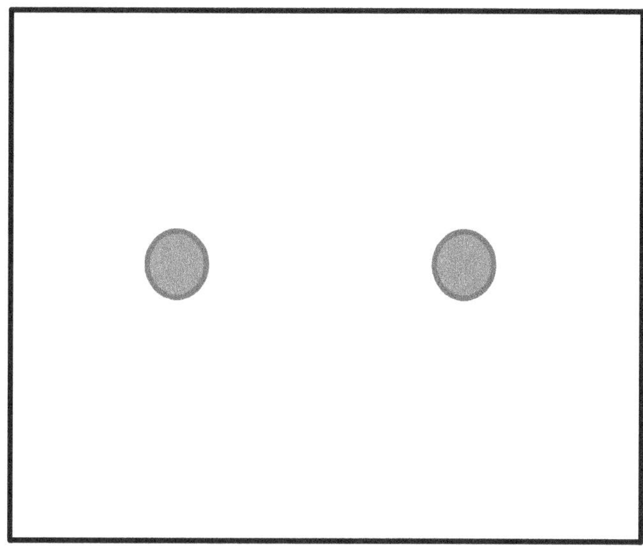

Figure 2. Finding Your Blind Spot

Another example can be found in the 1976 *Nature* article, “Hearing Lips and Seeing Voices,” in which authors Harry McGurk and John MacDonald describe the effect of vision on hearing.[8] The phenomenon has become known as the “McGurk Effect,” and we can see this on numerous internet videos simply by searching on that term.[9] McGurk and MacDonald showed what happens when a soundtrack consisting of a series of pursed mouth sounds (*ba-ba-ba*) is synchronized with a video of an individual mouthing a series of open-mouthed sounds (*ga-ga-ga*). Most of us will hear something like *da-da-da*. When we close our eyes, however, we hear the *ba-ba-ba* soundtrack. The effect varies somewhat with language, and it is typically strongest when the sound is a bit corrupted. Hearing and seeing did not evolve separately, and somewhere along the line our brains decided that hearing is not just what our ears do.

While retinal blind spots and visual effects on hearing are fairly subtle, other deceptions border on the absurd. Consider, for example, inattentional blindness, or the problem of looking without seeing. Daniel Simons and Chris Chabris vividly demonstrated this effect in a classic experiment done at Harvard University and later published in *Perception* in 1999.[10] They asked subjects to watch a video tape of two teams playing a game. One team was dressed in white shirts and one in black. Each team of three players passed an orange basketball from one member of their team to another. The test subjects were asked to count the number of times the ball was passed from one white-shirted individual to another.

The trick was that for about 5 seconds of the 75-second video, an actor dressed in a black gorilla suit wandered through the middle of the two teams while they were passing the balls. After the test, the observers were asked a series of questions to see if they noticed anything unusual. More than half of the subjects never saw the actor in the gorilla suit while they were focused on counting the ball passes. Their brains simply didn't think that the gorilla was important enough to the task at hand.

We Are a Jumble of Biases

A bias is systematic error that leads us in one direction or another. It is different from an error that is random. If we had a balance or scale that consistently reported weights that were 2 ounces heavier than actual, for example, we would say that the scale had a bias of plus 2 ounces.

Biases also exist as prejudices or influences that affect our thinking. And just as we have a physical blind spot in our retina, we also can have a blind spot toward many of our own biases. The best that we can probably do is to try to understand what biases look like and adapt accordingly.

There are on the order of a hundred different types of biases, and many popular books have been written about them and how they lead to poor decisions.[11] I've included a list of examples and short descriptions of some of these biases in Appendix A. They are worth a quick review, if for no other reason than to develop some humility.

If I had to pick only three that really matter in critical decision making, they would be confirmation bias, anchoring, and rosy retrospections.

Confirmation bias. This is the tendency to reinforce what we already believe with additional supporting information, while at the same time, discounting or ignoring information that tends to refute it. Clearly, we cannot expect to understand an issue and make a good decision if we only pay attention to information that supports what we already want to believe. Without understanding the alternatives, we are in an intellectual rut.

Good decision-making depends on knowing when and how to change direction. We need to be receptive to valid new information that contradicts our current view, and allow it to temper our thoughts and actions. Otherwise:

- We ignore the warning signs that our children are using drugs and alcohol.

- We see people who are not like us in a negative way.
- We are convinced that GMOs are the devil's work simply because they are not "natural."
- We avoid vaccinations for infectious disease because of unverified rumors.
- We can't understand why anyone should be allowed to own a gun.

A closed mind that only sees the same thing over and over again is intellectually dead. There is an old Mark Twain saying:[12]

> *Travel is fatal to prejudice, bigotry, and narrow-mindedness, and many of our people need it sorely on these accounts. Broad, wholesome, charitable views of men and things cannot be acquired by vegetating in one little corner of the earth all one's lifetime.*

While this statement is frequently heard on travelogues, it is essentially a general statement about taking in other perspectives and thus getting over confirmation bias.

Anchoring. Decisions and beliefs can be unduly influenced by first perceptions. In his book, *You are Not So Smart*, author David McRaney uses the example of a common sales trick in which the item we like is vastly overpriced, but just happens to be on sale the day we walk in the store. That first price tag ($1000) anchors us so that when we see the sale price of $400 (probably still way too much), we whip out a credit card without hesitation.[13]

The power of anchoring is well known in the media. For example, Simon Singh tells the story of a BBC documentary that described the practice of acupuncture. The presentation began with an open-heart surgery done in China that implied acupuncture was the only anesthetic used by the doctor. Clearly this gets our attention, and plants the idea that this ancient form of alternative medicine must go far beyond the placebo effect.[14] It took Singh quite a while to find the truth: that the patient was heavily sedated and had massive amounts of local anesthesia that negated the need for a general anesthetic. The needles that supposedly eliminated the pain were simply window dressing.[15]

Anchoring is a dangerous bias because it is often the first idea one is exposed to that becomes a foundation that can be difficult to shake. A poor first impression, for example, is often hard to recover from. Similarly, when facing an uncomfortable problem, we sometimes take the first solution that comes into our heads, and quit looking for better ones.

Rosy Retrospection. This is the tendency to remember the past as better than it actually was. For example, the 2016 Republican political campaign slogan *Make America Great Again* was an attempt to evoke this bias in voters who felt their lives and country were in decline. It was a great sound bite because it played to the rosy retrospection bias and voters didn't think too hard about it. What was left unsaid, however, was that living in the America-that-was-so-great was, in fact, far from perfect, and today's America is far better in many respects.[16] The America of the 1950s-1970s was not a nice place for many of the people who lived there. The air and water were filthy. Medical practice was often rudimentary. The Vietnam and Korean Wars left more than 94,000 U.S. military dead.[17] Poverty rates for the elderly were far higher than today. There were riots and burning of cities. Women were more blatantly discriminated against in employment. Racism and segregation were more commonplace. And there was also the tiny issue of global thermonuclear war to worry about. Yet many people forgot those realities.

We Make Too Many Logical Errors

Just as we can make errors in mathematics, such as adding 2 plus 2 and getting 8, we can also make errors in reasoning that can undercut our conclusions. We call these logical errors or logical fallacies.

One very powerful logical error that occurs frequently is the *appeal to popularity*, or the argument that someone should do something simply because others are doing it. The form is quite simple:

Everyone is doing X,
So, X must be the right thing to do.

When someone uses this form of false logic, they are just accepting someone else's behavior as right, without looking at the evidence.

This fallacy is the subject of Charles MacKay's *Extraordinary Popular Delusions and the Madness of Crowds.*[18] Written in 1841, this book addresses a variety of historical financial disasters in which people invested in wild schemes because they saw others doing the same thing. One example is the tulip mania that took place in 17th century Holland, where the prices of tulips were bid to ridiculous levels. Eventually, this business frenzy ended, causing financial ruin to many.

While we might think this fallacy is quaint and a relic of the past, it is not something we have outgrown as we have become more sophisticated investors. The same effect occurred in the dot-com stock market bubble that lasted from 1995 to 2000 in the U.S. This tech bubble was a period of irrational speculation about the growth and potential of the internet and the world wide web. Ridiculous valuations were placed on questionable internet business ideas and investors couldn't wait to get a piece of the action. One person's tulip is another's *pets.com.* [19]

Here are some additional logical errors that show up frequently and are relatively easy to spot. We've all probably been guilty of them at some point.

When someone uses an insult as if it was part of a valid argument.[20] In the most recent presidential election, for example, immaterial attacks on a candidate's appearance, character or personality were often substituted for rational debate. Why argue the merits of ideas when you can just call your opponent a "*%$@#!*/*" and score votes that way? Such mudslinging can influence the average voter, but we are far better off dismissing the tactic and perhaps dinging the candidate who resorts to them.

When someone argues that something is true because Einstein or Ben Franklin said it was.[21] Referencing someone like Albert Einstein or Benjamin Franklin when making a point is an attempt to convey an authority that is accepted and not questioned. Advertising does the same sort of thing when marketers make claims like "More doctors smoke Camel cigarettes than any other brand," (a 1940s ad) or they select a well-respected actor to pitch an insurance or mortgage product. (a 2020 ad)

We often create our own infallible authorities. Many, for example, blindly accept something because it was reported on their favorite web site or said by their favorite commentator. Whom we choose to read or listen to is one of the biggest decisions we have to make in determining what we know and how we know it. A good rule of thumb is to never blindly accept anything important, no matter who might have said it.

When the absence of evidence is considered as evidence. If we can't find evidence of something, that lack can suggest that something is false or does not exist, but it isn't proof. Similarly, you can't state with certainty that something is true simply because there is no evidence that it is false. It is easy to make such claims, but often time consuming and expensive to refute them. *Prove me wrong* is not an argument that something is true, yet it is widely used by some advertisers and conspiracy advocates.[22]

Arguing that a preceding incident caused a later one.[23] If someone performs a ritual and it rains, that doesn't mean that the ritual caused the rain. Or if someone prayed for success in the Powerball lottery and won, that does not mean prayer is a good Powerball strategy. On the other hand, if we change the oil in our car and the motor burns up shortly from lack of oil because we forgot to tighten the drain plug, it is pretty safe to say that our mistake caused the disaster. What matters is the evidence for cause and effect, not simply the before/after sequence in time.

Applying different criteria to different sides of an argument. If we apply different standards to different sides of an argument, then we are inconsistent. One often sees this error, for example, in how some react to advertising for weight-loss products. Ads often rely on carefully selected before-and-after pictures to convince us that taking the magic pill will let us eat whatever we want and still lose weight. In the end, many buyers will consider the before-and-after pictures more compelling than the overwhelming amount of scientific evidence demonstrating that there is no silver bullet for dieting. The decision to buy is based on a lower quality of evidence than the decision not to buy.

Use of false analogies. An analogy is a comparison of two things that are similar in some ways. We use them a great deal to understand things that we don't really know. How many times, for example, have we heard "it is a bit like...," or "it is similar to...," or "you can think of it as...?" Unfortunately, some analogies are better than others and the weak ones can often lead to poor conclusions.

The effectiveness of an analogy depends on understanding the ways in which the analogous items are alike and dissimilar and their relevance to the issue at hand. For example, teaching students that an atom is like a solar system with a nucleus (sun) and electrons (planets) is one simple way to get them started, but the analogy quickly falls apart when discussions of quantum mechanics begin.

These seven examples are only a few of the many different types of logical fallacies that exist. I have compiled a list of some of them in Appendix B.[24] It is worth a few minutes of study to get a feel for some of the fallacies that often plague our thinking.

There are many, many ways that we can commit logical fallacies. And short of a PhD in Philosophy, most of us are unlikely to get them right all of the time. The real message of the list is that a little humility is warranted when we think through a problem. Our arguments likely have more holes in them than we might want to believe.

Our Memories Often Fail Us

Neuroscientists tell us that the human brain has about 86 billion neurons and on the order of 10^14 connections among them.[25] If we assume that each connection or synapse can store 1 byte of data, this would imply a capacity of on the order of 100 terabytes.[26] To put this number in perspective, let's assume that our brains are like digital video recorders. We would need to stream *Star Trek* or *Hill Street Blues* or *The Price is Right* 24 hours a day, 7 days a week, and 365 days per year, for about 12 years in order to fill our brains with the details of these stories. [27]

Our brains are not like digital video recorders, however. Instead, we encode and store information about events in various parts of the brain, and then reconstruct the events. For the most part, this works fine for the day-to-day situations we face. But these reconstructions are all subject to our biases and logical fallacies.

Some of the most tragic examples of memory failure are inaccurate eyewitness testimony. Elizabeth Loftus, professor at the University of California at Irvine has studied how peoples' memories become corrupted and has consulted with police in hundreds of criminal cases. In her words, "Just because somebody tells you something and they say it with confidence. Just because they say it with lots of detail. Just because they express emotion when they say it. It doesn't mean that it really happened."[28]

One clue that we tend to reconstruct memories can be seen when psychologists ask subjects to memorize a series of words associated with a particular subject. When asked to repeat the list, the subjects often recall words that weren't in the list but are part of the category. For example, if the series of words to remember was: fish, cats, mice, gerbils, hamsters, parakeets, guinea pigs, hedgehogs, ferrets, and rabbits, subjects might also include dogs in their recall.

As Daniel Kahneman notes in *Thinking Fast and Slow*, "our experiencing selves and our remembering selves perceive things differently."[29]

We Think We Understand Better Than We Do

In general, we overestimate how much we know about a subject. Psychologists call this the illusion of explanatory depth.

Cal Tech physicist Richard Feynman liked to tell a story about South Pacific islanders and the Cargo Cult Culture that arose after WWII. During the war, the U.S. constructed aircraft runways on remote islands in order to help defeat the Japanese. The inhabitants of the island saw what happened, but had no understanding of what they saw:

> *During the war they saw airplanes land with lots of good materials, and they want the same thing to happen now. So, they've arranged to make things like runways, to put fires along the sides of the runways, to make a wooden hut for a man to sit in, with two wooden pieces on his head like headphones and bars of bamboo sticking out like antennas—he's the controller—and they wait for the airplanes to land. They're doing everything right. The form is perfect. It looks exactly the way it looked before.*[30]

The islanders knew nothing but the most superficial aspects of communications and logistics, just what things looked like on the surface and how its operators acted. That became the basis for their actions.

While we might be prone to laugh at this lack of sophistication, we do the same thing despite our so-called worldliness. For example, many of us are as clueless as the cargo cult people with respect to much of our current technology. And while we don't slap pieces of wood on the sides of our heads, we do something just as simplistic — we memorize and parrot explanations.

For example, we have all heard of E = mc^2. It rolls easily off our tongues. We might even be able to say that E is energy, m is mass and c is the speed of light. But what does any of that really mean? How did Einstein arrive at it? How does it relate to relativity? What does it tell us about the universe? How is it practical? We can smugly parrot E=mc^2, but most of are simply slapping coconut shells on our ears when it comes to any useful depth of understanding.[31]

The illusion of explanatory depth was driven home to me most forcefully when I was a young college professor teaching materials engineering. I dutifully tested my students every week on facts and basic calculations related to the subject, and they seemed to generally get it. That belief held until I tried an experiment. Instead of simply asking for a calculation involving a specific relationship, I blended two simple problems together. While the students had no trouble with the simple individual problems, very few of them could make the leap to linking the two together. This suggested to me that they were memorizing not just facts, but solutions as well, rather than understanding the ideas and relationships. Needless to say, I changed my teaching strategy.

Unfortunately, people who are the poorest performers tend to overestimate their abilities the most. This result is a component of the so-called Dunning-Kruger effect that appears in many everyday life experiences. Dunning and Kruger summarize the effect nicely in their classic paper, "Unskilled and Unaware of It: How Difficulties in Recognizing One's Own Incompetence Lead to Inflated Self-Assessments":

> *People tend to hold overly favorable views of their abilities in many social and intellectual domains...this overestimation occurs, in part, because people who are unskilled in these domains suffer a dual burden: Not only do these people reach erroneous conclusions and make unfortunate choices, but their incompetence robs them of the metacognitive ability to realize it.*[32]

Those who lack ability do not perform well, but along with that lack of ability and poor performance comes a belief that they are far more capable than they really are. Anyone who has had to give performance reviews as part of their job probably understands this effect.

No one is immune to the Dunning-Kruger effect. When we find ourselves at odds with others' assessments or believing that we know better than those who are truly expert in a field, it is time for a closer look. My favorite example is a study done with the faculty at the University of Nebraska. As teachers, 68% rated themselves in the top 25%, and more than 90% rated themselves above average.[33]

We Take Too Much Pride in Common Sense

We all love common sense. Telling someone that they have good common sense is considered one of the nicest of compliments. We even poke fun at the lack of common sense with contests like the Darwin Awards that honor the most outrageously stupid stunts imaginable. These often involve statements like: *Here, light this fuse*, or *Hold my beer and watch this*. One of the key criteria for winning the award is that the individual must exhibit "outstanding misapplication of judgement."[34]

Webster says common sense is "sound judgment derived from experience rather than study." The Oxford dictionary says: "good sense and sound judgment in practical matters." Both imply it is a positive trait that requires a grounding in practical experiences rather than theory, and an ability to learn from one's experiences.

The danger of common sense is that it is frequently used as a substitute for real knowledge or expertise in decision making. Whatever mental models our prior experience and study create will eventually fail us when they don't cover what we are currently experiencing and the context in which we experience it. Here is an example of a problem that is likely unfamiliar and illustrates the danger of the limits of experience and common sense.

Consider the mechanical puzzle in Figure 3 that is a specific configuration of springs, weights, and wires. The *zig-zags* represent two identical springs that stretch proportionally when weight is added and contract proportionally when weight is removed. The lines represent wires that cannot stretch or contract significantly. The two outer wires are loose and the middle wire is taut.

In your experience, what would happen if you cut the middle wire? Does the weight move up or down? Most of us will say that the weight will drop when the wire is cut. It is only common sense that something should drop when we remove its support.

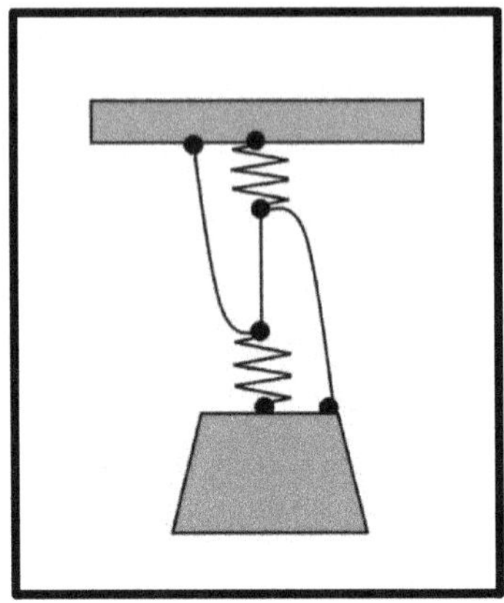

Figure 3. Spring-Mass System: What Happens If You Cut the Middle Wire?

Except that in this case, the weight can go either up or down. To begin to see why, we have to go to a less familiar level of thinking and understanding. Picture the weight in two conditions, one with the middle wire intact and one with it severed. Cutting the wire changes the configuration. The weight originally supported by the two springs in series (one right after the other in a line) is now supported by these same two springs in parallel (side-by-side). Each spring is now supporting only half of the weight and will contract (pull up) as a result. Figure 4 shows the configurations before and after the middle wire is cut.[35]

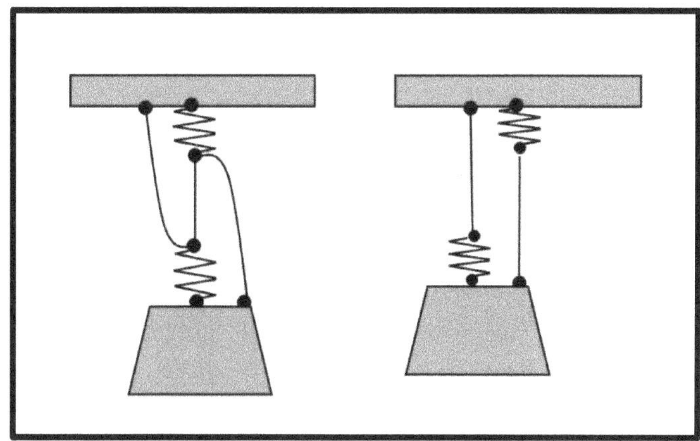

Figure 4. Before-and-After Configuration of Spring-Mass System

The correct answer is sometimes that the weight moves upward, but not always. Whether the weight rises, falls, or remains at the original height for a given set of weight and springs also depends on the lengths of the wires. If the wires are too long, for example, they will allow the weight to drop too far, and the contraction of the springs will not be able to compensate for all of the drop.[36]

For most observers, common sense will mislead them with this puzzle. At the first level, *what goes up must come down* fails us. At the second level, one can fail to understand the somewhat obscure notion that cutting the wire completely changes the nature of the support. And at the third level, one's intuition can easily fail to grasp the nature of the sensitivity to wire length.

Relying on common sense is insufficient and far too simplistic to make the correct decision in this case. In addition, the example illustrates that it is often dangerous to stop at the first level of thought in a decision just because it seems to make sense.

Most of the difficult problems that we face require going far beyond the obvious. But this doesn't mean that we discard common sense. It is just that it is often not enough. Sometimes we have to learn something new (like mass-spring behavior). And that often involves discarding or modifying cherished beliefs that were long part of our common sense.

There is an old saying that science had to be invented because common sense is so often wrong. Just like the simple spring-mass problem, applying only our limited common sense to complex topics like climate change, government, economics, health, politics, and even many aspects of human behavior will often lead us astray.

Our Emotions and Desires Can Override Rational Thinking

In his novel, *The Jungle*, Upton Sinclair wrote that "it is difficult to get a man to understand something when his salary depends on not understanding it." *The Jungle* was a fictional expose of the meat packing industry that publicly revealed some of the terrible work conditions and practices in that industry during the early 1900s. Sinclair's point was that we can rationalize anything that we have a stake in.[37]

We might think that a better approach is to always keep emotions out of decisions. Perhaps everyone should be like Mr. Spock on the television show *Star Trek*. But like many things in this world, emotion is a mixed blessing. Most of the critical decisions that we make in life are made with incomplete information and some degree of uncertainty. In such cases, logic alone is inadequate and we have to rely to some degree on emotion, if only for our tolerance of risk. On the other hand, we all know from experience that emotions can sometimes mislead us. In making decisions, therefore, it helps to know when we are being played.

Emotional manipulation is common, for example, in tv ads for good causes. These ads are almost always loaded with powerful images and testimonials. An ad that seeks funding to help abused animals inevitably includes a small pitiful dog shaking in fear. Similarly, ads seeking funding for disadvantaged children always include some of the cutest kids ever. The producers of these ads want us to act without considering questions such as how much money the charity siphons off for administration and fundraising, or how much of a difference a particular charity's efforts really makes, or whether another charity is more worthy.[38]

Emotions also sometimes prevent us from seeing alternative views or perspectives. This is particularly the case in politics. For example, some of my acquaintances absolutely hate President Donald Trump and everything he stands for. While I am not a big fan of his, I recognize that it would be pretty hard to be in the most powerful position on earth and not do something good. So, I challenged my friends to come up with one thing that President Trump did during his first two years in office that helped the country. So far, they've come up with nothing. Not because he had done no good, but because they are somewhat blinded by their emotions. I'm sure that had I asked some of my ardent Republican friends the same question about the Obama administration a few years earlier, I would have gotten the same result.

We Look for Black and White in a Gray World

When the time comes to find a solution to a problem, we often rely on sound bites — the worst form of black and white — to describe our thoughts. This is especially obvious, for example, in the issue of gun control:

> *A good man with a gun is the best solution to a bad man with a gun.*
> *The only way to get rid of gun violence is to get rid of guns.*

Significant portions of the U.S. population cling to these extreme positions. In their view, there is no reasonable compromise between weapons being largely unnecessary for most of the population and believing that they are the only real solution to protecting one's family from criminals and a government that is not to be trusted.

Most of the world is gray and we are far better off trying to understand all sides of an issue than simply choosing one side or another. Are any of these sound bites familiar?

- My religion is the one true religion.
- All (liberals or conservatives) are clueless.
- I hate math.
- You can't trust big business.

- Lying is always wrong.
- All politicians are crooks.

Positions like these do not solve problems or lead to good ideas. They only polarize, and when those beliefs turn to action, people often get hurt. Perhaps we'd all a bit better off if we headed for the middle ground, rather than what we perceive as the high ground.

We All Have a Bit of the Conspiracy Buff in Us

In the fall of 2018, a disgruntled Floridian who strongly supported President Trump began sending explosive devices through the mail to some of the President's strongest critics. This person had a long history of criminal activity and psychological problems. Fortunately, no one was hurt.

His timing was great, however, with the mid-term elections only a few weeks away, and this gave the conspiracy buffs plenty of time to speculate. My favorite was courtesy of a neighbor of mine, whose friend (and ardent Trump supporter) claimed rather emotionally that the whole thing was a Democratic scheme to make Trump and his followers look bad.

Democrats have their share of conspiracy theorists, too, of course. During the 2018 hearings for Brett Kavanaugh's appointment to the Supreme Court, rumors flew about on social media that Russia had bailed Kavanaugh (who was not popular with Democrats), out of debt.[39]

We all love a good conspiracy, and for some, it doesn't matter whether there is any real evidence to support it. The believers want it to be true and they will hang onto anything that might feed that belief.

Over the years, there have been some truly amazing conspiracy theories:

- American astronauts never landed on the moon.
- A secret society known as the *Illuminati* really controls the world.
- The government controls populations by putting a strong tranquilizer (the fluoride added to prevent tooth decay) in the public water supply.
- The Defense Department created Lyme disease as a biological weapon.[40]
- Alien remains are stored at Area 51, where the government reverse engineers their advanced technology.[41]

And while government is often a dominant theme in conspiracy, industry is also a favorite target.[42]

- Paul McCartney really died in 1966 and was replaced by a lookalike.
- The Coca-Cola company introduced *New Coke* as a ploy to increase sales of the original formula.
- The BP oil spill was perpetrated by environmentalists as a way to halt drilling in the Gulf of Mexico.
- Pharmaceutical companies created the 2014 Ebola epidemic in order to profit from vaccines.

- Ultra-high efficiency car technologies have been suppressed by oil companies in order to feed profits.

While we might tend to think of conspiracy thinking as a fringe activity, it really isn't. According to researchers at the University of Chicago, for example, "half of the American public consistently endorses at least one conspiracy theory."[43] Popular web applications like YouTube have become a favorite way of spreading such theories.

Webster defines a conspiracy theory as "a theory that explains an event or set of circumstances as the result of a secret plot by usually powerful conspirators."[44] And while some theories have turned out to be true (the CIA did experiment with mind-control drugs; and companies really did hide the risk of smoking from the public, for example), most are just fiction.

Some conspiracy theories are harmless. Who really cares whether their brother-in-law thinks that the U.S. did not land on the moon or that aliens landed at Roswell? But others can have deadly consequences, like refusing to vaccinate school children because of a belief in an anti-vaccine conspiracy theory.[45]

The trick to evaluating conspiracies is to keep separate what we would like to believe is true from what is likely true. Noted skeptic, Michael Shermer, provides a nice list of clues to help identify false conspiracy theories. Here they are in abbreviated form:[46]

- The conspiracy connects events that are likely unrelated or have other non-conspiratorial explanations.
- The conspiracy requires extraordinary power and influence to pull off.
- The conspiracy is complex.
- The conspiracy involves a lot of people who would need to keep quiet.
- The conspiracy suggests world domination.
- The conspiracy takes small events and blows them up into much larger and less probable events.
- The conspiracy suggests sinister meanings to what are more likely innocuous events.
- The theory mixes facts and speculation, without any distinction between the two.
- The conspiracy is built on a suspicion of all government agencies or private groups.
- The conspiracy is confirmation biased; that is, the believer only believes information that confirms the conspiracy theory.

Shermer notes that the more these characteristics fit the conspiracy theory, the less likely it is going to be true. If someone is one of the remaining few who seriously believe that climate change is just a government hoax, for example, they might benefit from objectively reviewing what brought them to that conclusion, in light of Shermer's criteria.

Some Warning Signs

Politics can drive us all a bit crazy at times, and thus can be fertile ground for testing our critical thinking skills and the actions we take as a result. As an example, we should all take a good look at our own politics. Here are some signs that we might not be thinking as well as we could:

- We only vote the party line without considering the other candidates.
- We've changed our vote just to be on the winning side.
- We've voted for or against something that we didn't understand.
- We didn't vote in an election because we thought it wasn't worth the trouble.
- We never registered to vote or we let our registration lapse.
- Our only information about a voting decision came from a billboard or TV ad.
- We made a voting decision without consulting sources that provide fact checking.
- We voted for someone because of their appearance. For example, one candidate was tall and their opponent was short.
- We made a voting decision based on a political action committee ad.
- Someone paid us to vote a certain way.
- We voted for or against someone based on a single issue, and paid no attention to positions on other issues.

- We accidently voted for someone whose name was similar to someone else's.
- We voted for the first person listed because it was easier than studying the candidates.
- We voted for someone because they shook our hand.

If anyone answered no to all of these questions, I have only one thing to say: liar, liar, pants on fire!

The Bottom Line

Despite what we would all like to believe, we are flawed thinkers. Any confidence that you or I have in our ability to objectively think through a particular problem might not be completely warranted.

Chris Wood, a former vice president at the Santa Fe Institute, put it this way:

> *We are not rational beings at our heart....We are characterized by a whole suite of (in many cases, unconscious, and in some cases, completely inaccessible by us) biases and predilections that come out of our evolutionary history and its interaction with our environment that lead us to behave in quite unpredictable ways, frequently departing quite extensively from what one would expect of a rational actor.*[47]

But that is no reason to be completely disillusioned. Don't fall into the trap of thinking that our decisions must always be perfect. The world is largely gray, and some important decisions can be better or worse, without being right or wrong in some absolute sense.

CHAPTER TWO

How the World Exploits Our Weaknesses

Ignorance more frequently begets confidence than does knowledge— Charles Darwin

We live in a world that constantly deceives us. These acts of deception can be largely or completely unconscious, such as the camouflage or mimicry that evolves in insects and animals. Or they can be blatantly deliberate, like the confidence game that seeks to separate us from our money. By better understanding how deception is used to influence our decisions, we can become more effective at dealing with the enticements that are thrown at us every day.

Deception

One clue to the pervasiveness of deception in our lives is the extensive vocabulary that has evolved to describe it. In the

English language, there are well over 100 different terms for deception. Table 1 is just the C's and D's.[48]

• Camouflage	• Deceit
• Cheating	• Delusion
• Collusion	• Denial
• Confabulation	• Double Dealing
• Conjuring	• Double Cross
• Cunning	• Duplicity
• Con	• Dissembling

Table 1. Some English Words for Deception (Cs & Ds)

Some of the terms are very general (like cheating) while others can sometimes mean very specific forms of deception (for example, conjuring can mean to call upon a spirit).

As noted earlier, deception can occur in all of nature. But people seem particularly good at it. Do any of these examples seem familiar?

- Interpersonal relationships (*I would never lie to you.*)
- The legal profession (*My client was just holding those drugs for a friend.*)
- Sports and games (*Don't count that one!)*
- The insurance industry (*Do you want the extended warranty?)*
- The cosmetic industry (*The wrinkles are gone in just three days!)*
- Marketing and sales (*Sign here and here and here. The 15-pages of fine print are just boiler plate.*)

- Computing (*Hi, I'm Ted calling from Microsoft about a problem with your computer.*)
- Politics (*It depends on what the meaning of the word "is" is.*)

These examples suggest that what we see and hear are the most common venues used to deceive us. But deception can be more generally defined as the act of misleading or wrongly informing someone about the true nature of a situation.[49] Thus a well-executed deception plan can target any of our basic senses, not just what we are hearing or seeing.[50] For example: spices in food can be used to hide a myriad of bad smells and tastes; and the feel of a well-counterfeited twenty-dollar bill can fool us into thinking it is genuine currency.

Not Everyone Is as Honest as You Are

According to Canadian criminologist Thomas Gabor, people are rarely honest or dishonest all of the time.[51] The majority of us fall in the middle — sometimes a saint and sometimes a sinner. Where we are at any given time depends on the circumstances.

Why do people act dishonestly? There are many reasons, but one frequent cause is a sense of unfairness. Tax fraud, for example, is often rationalized by the belief that the tax system is rigged for the rich, and that the government just wastes the money anyway. Other times, pressure to succeed pushes people over the edge. In their minds, the end justifies the means. Others just like the idea of getting away with something, or having someone else pay their fair share for them. And, of course, many believe that *everyone is doing it* and *you have to do it to get ahead*, are sufficiently compelling rationalizations to justify dishonest acts.[52]

We are really good at rationalizing our own bad behavior, overestimating our honesty, and minimizing the wrongness of our past deeds. Psychologists often refer to this effect as the *fundamental attribution error*. When we do something wrong, we blame it on circumstances. When others act poorly, it is because of bad character.[53] This is one example of a more general theme in which we are far better at spotting flaws in others than in ourselves.

Deception Can Take Subtle Forms

Deceptions are not always bald-faced lies, blatant violations of rules, or out-and-out swindles. Most forms of deceit are far more subtle. For instance:

Deception often hides in what is not said. The real estate agent neglects to tell us about the neighbor's fondness for drugs and alcohol. A scientist neglects to disclose that he takes money from the company making the drug that he is researching. A child fails to mention that there will be no parental supervision at the party he or she is attending. Proponents of a cause neglect counter arguments as they selectively choose facts to build a case. We neglect to mention that we were texting when the accident occurred.

Deception often hides in exaggeration or downplay. Taxpayers exaggerate deductions and hide income.[54] A job applicant's resume is somewhat embellished. We really don't get as much exercise as we tell the doctor. We drive quite a few more miles each year than we put on the automobile insurance form.

Deception often hides in how something is said or written. Political speeches and news reports are filled with trigger words designed to inflame or incite. The side effects of drugs are in print that is too small to read or said so quickly that no one hears them. An insurance policy or apartment lease is a lengthy morass of legalese that no one bothers to read. Inaccurate statements are repeated frequently with no explanation in order to get listeners to believe them without thinking.

Deception often hides in how something or someone is presented. A homeowner puts a coat of paint on the house he is selling to hide that bit of decay or water stains. A gang member who is accused of murder shows up in court for trial with a conservative haircut and a new suit that conveniently covers offensive tattoos. The garage mechanic squirts a little hydraulic fluid on our car's shock absorbers before telling us that they need to be replaced.

As Deborah Rhode notes in her insightful book, *Cheating: Ethics in Everyday Life*: "The vast majority of everyday cheating lacks moral justifications. The conduct persists because so many individuals see the benefits as much more tangible, immediate, and compelling than the costs."[55]

It's a wonder we survive! Or perhaps we survive because of it?

Caveat Emptor

Caveat emptor is a Latin term for *let the buyer beware.* It essentially puts the onus on buyers to make sure they are getting what they believe they are buying.

Sellers work hard to separate us from our money, and they have many ways to manipulate a potential consumer. Do any of these seem familiar?[56]

- The muscled hunk riding the exercise machine in the gym advertisement.
- The Super PAC ad loaded with unflattering pictures of the opponent or content-free slogans like *Vote NO on Proposition* 1.
- The lawyer or law firm trolling for accident victims, with the suggestion of large settlements.
- Drugs advertised as *new and improved* that are sometimes no better or worse than older cheaper drugs.
- The light-beer commercial in which everyone is happy, healthy, active, and lean.
- The pop-up ad offering a great promotion on a product that, coincidently, we were just surfing a few days ago.
- The online game we just can't resist playing for hours on end.
- The like button on Facebook.
- The service agreement change that begins with *in order to serve you better.*

Cosmetics executive Charles Revson was once quoted as saying that "In the factory we make cosmetics, in the store we sell hope."[57] Essentially, all of the above examples are selling hope in some way or another, playing on our biases and our desires for reward and fear of losing out. When we are tempted by these ads, we should ask: *how am I being manipulated?* This is an essential part of the process of answering the larger issue of *what do I know and how do I know it*?

Good references for learning some of the tricks of advertising and ways in which technology is being used to manipulate us are: (1) Paco Underhill's *Why We Buy: The Science of Shopping*, and (2) Adam Alter's *Irresistible: The Rise of Addictive Technology and the Business of Keeping Us Hooked.* There are good reasons, for example, why Steve Jobs and other technical leaders did not allow their children unlimited access to tools like iPads.[58]

One of the better protections against seriously deceptive advertising is to look to the Federal Trade Commission, or FTC. You can sign up for their scam alert service at https://www.ftc.gov. This service covers a wide range of topics, such as these that appeared around the time of this writing:

- Deceptive stem cell therapy claims
- Bogus diabetes treatment claims
- Romance scams
- Bogus product claims related to losing weight
- Executive placement scams
- Quick-fix scams for credit
- The dangers of free trial offers

Most importantly, we don't need a PhD and the patience of Job to understand these alerts. They are short and written in plain English.

Phone and Computer Scams

We receive a great deal of value and enjoyment from the phones and computers that are now a central part of our daily lives and decision making. But these features of civilization also bring with them a host of threats to our health, welfare, time, and wallets.

For the moment, imagine that we are being targeted by a con artist who wants to influence us in some way. That person could be an identity thief who wants our Social Security number, an IRS impersonator who wants us to send them money, a *GoFundMe* site that wants funds for less-than-honorable reasons, or a hacker who wants to install ransomware on our computer. Their success or failure depends on three things:

- What they bring to the table.
- How the environment provides opportunity.
- What the target (we) bring to the table.

By examining each of these, we can see a bit more about how con artists work, understand the unique opportunities for deception that these highly connected services provide, and determine where our weak points lie. These, in turn, might help us make better decisions in a world where more and more of our decision making is no longer face-to-face.

What the con man brings. The entry fee for effective schemes based on the internet and other digital phenomena clearly includes some skill and knowledge about computers, social media, and related technologies. But mostly it just requires extending the skills that have always been needed to run a good scam.

An effective con man must be good at gaining our confidence, and this can sometimes be easier to do on the internet than face to face.[59] A teenager who would never get into a van with a stranger might willingly establish an online relationship with an unknown person who "really understands them." An official-looking notice from the bank saying that there is a problem with our account sometimes causes enough angst to get us to click the link and reenter our account information. Or someone on Craigslist feigns interest in the car we are selling and robs us when we get together for the transaction. Without the cues of face-to-face encounters, it can be much easier for scammers to play their role.

Of course, good scammers know about our biases and have ways to get us to let down our guard whether we are on a phone or online. A common trick is to get us to panic and react without thinking. Robocalls, for example, often start with something like *enforcement agencies have suspended your social security number*, or *an arrest warrant has been issued in your name.* Scammers also like to play on our laziness, greed, or lack of time. This is why so-called "dark patterns" meant to steer or coerce us are so popular in web page design.[60] If we take the bait, we become a puppet whose strings are pulled with predictable results.

How the digital environment provides opportunity for cons. The internet and digital commerce provide unprecedented opportunities to deceive and cheat others. Here are some examples of the capabilities that this new world provides:

- Easy access to a vast reserve of personal information about potential targets. The time has long passed, for example, when we had to go to the county recorder's office or the telephone company to get information about someone.
- The ability to purchase confidential information like credit cards and social security numbers on the dark web. Tools like the Tor browser, for example, guarantee anonymity in such illegal activities.[61]
- Widespread availability of hacking tools. *John the Ripper*, for example, is a readily-available open source tool used to crack passwords.
- A world wide web that is more concerned about seamless market transactions than security. In fairness, however, there is always a balance between security and convenience.
- The ability to work anywhere in the world and obscure an identity and a physical location. Even if the cybercrime folks at the FBI can find you in some foreign country, they generally do not have arrest authority.[62]

But perhaps the most insidious aspect of internet and phone cons is the ability to reach millions of potential victims with relatively little effort and investment. With such large numbers, playing low percentages becomes very profitable. A fake lottery scheme, for example, works because one only needs a small percentage of clueless people to respond. It cost almost nothing to send out any number of emails or robocalls. On the other hand, if someone had to stuff envelopes and lick stamps, such schemes would be far less efficient and effective.[63]

What the target brings. People's habits, knowledge, experience, and mental state all contribute to their susceptibility. There is much for a con man to exploit:

- Laziness: such as taking advantage of a convenient open WiFi network to make an online purchase or check a bank account.
- Lack of computer knowledge: such as continuing to use an obsolete computer whose security features are no longer effective.
- Carelessness: such as leaving an unprotected cell phone in a cab or restaurant, or using weak passwords on computers.
- Age: the elderly are typically less savvy about new technologies, and the circumstances of aging sometimes diminish rational thought.
- Greed: an eagerness to believe something that is too good to be true.
- Fear: particularly of the Internal Revenue Service, threatening bill collectors, and the police.
- Gullibility: we are all a bit of a sucker for a sob story or anything else that we want to believe.
- Naivete: we innocently put sensitive information (like pictures of our children or travel plans) on Facebook.

- Lack of self-control: such as knowingly visiting questionable sites, or starting arguments on the internet with people we don't know.

It's hard to imagine a better time to be a con man. But the size of that bullseye on our computers and phones depends on whether we are going to rely on our gut or take the time to think critically about the data we are about to share or the button we are about to push. Knowing what con men are trying to accomplish, lowering our profiles, and protecting our technology are keys to improving the odds that our internet will be a source of information and enjoyment, not a gateway for the underworld to exploit our bad decisions.

More and more, we have to rely on software and hardware that are beyond the average person's comprehension, and assume that someone else is protecting our interests. But there is only so much that the industry can do to protect us from things like: *Hello, my name is Dave, and I am calling from Tech Russia about some problems with your computer.* On the internet, there is no better protection than repeatedly asking yourself what you know and how you know it.[64]

Elicitation

Every day, we are subjected to a variety of techniques intended to get us to tell others what they want to know. This process is known as elicitation, and while it is often beneficial and usually harmless, it is not always so. If we want to avoid decisions that we will later regret, it helps to understand a bit about how this technique works.

We might ask why anyone would willingly decide to admit something they shouldn't, but it happens frequently in casual chats with strangers, and even in more serious encounters like interviews and negotiations. In really good elicitation, we might not even remember what we said.

We are vulnerable to this type of information gathering because it is designed to exploit a range of our natural inclinations. According to the FBI, some of these include:[65]

- Appearing well-informed.
- Being polite and helpful.
- Feeling appreciated, and believing that we are contributing to something important.
- Showing off.
- Gossiping.
- Correcting others.
- Underestimating the value of the information being sought or given.
- Believing others to be honest.
- Answering a question truthfully.
- Converting others to our own opinion.

While we might not have a strong propensity toward all of these characteristics, we are all likely guilty of some of them.

Elicitors use a variety of tools to exploit these vulnerabilities, and get the information that they want. Appendix C contains a list of the more common ones. Here are three that can be especially effective.

Quid Pro Quo. Reciprocity is a very powerful instinct – you gave me something and I therefore feel that I owe you something. When someone shares personal information, for example, always be wary of the urge to reciprocate.

Encouraging the Urge to Complain. Many of us like to complain when we have a receptive audience. But if the urge hits us, we should always choose our audience carefully.

Feigning disbelief. Simply saying *I don't believe it* can bring on a wealth of new information. Many will feel the need to prove their statement, providing significant detail in the process.

Of course, there is more to elicitation than just a toolbox of techniques. As John Nolan, a former intelligence officer, notes in his book *Confidential: Uncover Your Competitors' Top Business Secrets Legally and Quickly--and Protect Your Own*, good elicitors design a conversation so that the key questions become less salient.[66] The important questions can't stick out or they will be remembered. Instead, they should be disguised as part of the conversation. General happy talk, followed by: *How often do you beat your children?*, is not going to work. Good elicitation will bury what is important in noise.

Elicitors work hard to establish trust. A hacker, for example, might pose as a company employee or contractor who is in a jam. By sharing company problems and knowledge, the hacker/elicitor tends to build camaraderie and sympathy that make their victim want to help. A few questions and comments to build sympathy, a bit of chit chat showing that they have some inside information, and the hacker quickly has the passcode he or she is seeking, just because we want to be helpful. As noted earlier, we can't easily eliminate this type of vulnerability with technology. The only effective strategy is awareness.

In the end, our best defense against elicitation is probably to just quit babbling on. Ask good questions, listen well, and learn to tolerate periods of silence. The Greek philosopher, Plato, is often credited with making the point this way: "Wise men speak because they have something to say; fools because they have to say something."[67]

Deception and Decisions

Decisions often involve people other than ourselves, and depending on how we decide an issue, some will benefit and others will lose. Whether it is someone on the phone trying to get our personal information, or a politician trying to get our vote, or a salesman trying to get us to buy the latest electronics *and* the optional five-year warranty, they will sometimes step over an ethical line. The potential for deception and subsequent poor decisions is greatest when those who benefit are providing the bulk of the information. Better decisions are made when we choose our inputs wisely.

CHAPTER THREE

Choosing Inputs Wisely

Millions of items of the outward order are present to my senses which never properly enter into my experience....My experience is what I agree to attend to.
— William James

A colleague of mine recently commented that we are not in the Information Age, but the Information *Overload* Age. We like to blame the internet and the world wide web for this problem, but it is really our choice to look at yet another cute cat video or otherwise wander aimlessly from one hyperlink to another.

In a sense, the problem today isn't that there is too much information, but rather that it is all too available and presented in a way that makes everything seem of equal merit. Anyone and everyone can create a tweet or a video or a blog or a website, and there is little control on the output.

We need to be careful about choosing what we read or listen to. What we feed our minds is a lot like what we feed our bodies. Are we looking for a steady mental diet of fast food or food that is good for us? As the 19th century philosopher William James wrote: "my experience is what I agree to attend to."[68]

It's Hard to Beat a Good Book

When trying to understand something complex that really matters, our best chance of success often lies with well-written and well-researched books. Why books and not someone's daily blog or web page? Simply because good books take a lot more time and effort to write. Also, most are written well after events occur, allowing time to filter out much of the hype and noise that inevitably cloud the near-term picture.[69]

But how do we tell if a book is worth reading? Here are some questions I try to answer before committing my time to any book I might learn from. They also apply to some extent to other sources of information like news networks, magazines, blogs, YouTube videos, Ted Talks, and other media.

What is author's background? Credentials and past performance matter. I will, for example, read anything that former Berkeley Physics Professor Richard Muller writes because he is widely recognized as one of the best teachers around. I'm bound to learn something useful from his books. When we don't know the author, on the other hand, YouTube videos, TED talks, and summary services like Blinkist can give us a better feel for the person and the book.[70] These online services can also be a quick way to get the key points of a book that you don't have time to commit to.

Is the book hyped in any way? Are there signs of deception? For example, claiming the existence of widespread conspiracy is a well-known strategy for getting attention. It is a common ploy in so-called "miracle cure" books whose authors claim that their low-cost solutions have been hidden or discredited by pharmaceutical and medical establishments that only care about profits.

Another clue that a book is hyped is the heavy use of trigger words and phrases. In the political literature, for example, look for terms and phrases like *political elite*, *take our country back*, *government handouts*, and *ghetto*. In alternative medicine, look for terms like *conspiracy*, *miracle cure, sacred, ancient,* and *limited supplies*. In nutrition, look for terms like: *poison*, *frankenfood*, and *all natural*. All of these suggest significant bias.

How extraordinary are the claims in the book? Remember the old saying that *extraordinary claims require extraordinary proof*. In particular, be wary of authors who cannot seem to tell the difference between an anecdote or testimonial and well-done research. Anecdotes and testimonials are not proof and they are frequently misleading and half-told. At best, they are a clue. At worst, they deceive.[71]

When scientific claims are made, check the original references. Such claims will often cite scientific research journals, but always consider the reputation of the journal. Some are far better than others. One important discriminant is how much influence the journal's articles have (the impact factor), as measured by the number of papers that cite them. Good scientists and engineers try to publish in journals with the highest impact factors.[72]

How diverse are the reviews? Who is writing about the book? Are the good reviews limited to those who are proponents of the topic, or do they include skeptics? Do the reviewers see strengths *and* weaknesses in the book? Reviewers who have a vested interest in the beliefs touted in the book will have a tough time seeing other points of view.

But keep in mind that reviews are opinion and, as such, can sometimes be way off of the mark. Perhaps the worst critical review ever written was done in 1863 by Oramel Barrett, a reporter for the Harrisburg, Pennsylvania newspaper. The review concerned President Lincoln's Gettysburg Address. Although Lincoln's address is arguably one of the most famous and moving speeches of all time, Barrett's review was as follows:

> *We pass over the silly remarks of the President. For the credit of the nation we are willing that the veil of oblivion shall be dropped over them and that they shall no more be repeated or thought of.*[73]

Clearly, one should always read more than one review. My guess is that Mr. Barrett voted for one of the other guys in the 1860 presidential election.

By answering the four questions in this section, we can learn a great deal about a book before reading it in detail. Sometimes this initial review will be all that we need and can decide that we don't need to invest many hours in a careful read. It's our time, so we should use it wisely.

We Don't Have to Read the Entire Book

William Casey was Director of Central Intelligence at the CIA from 1981 to 1987. He was quite a character and did not hesitate to tell anyone what he thought. At one point, he became concerned that his analysts were wasting too much time reading irrelevant or redundant material, and wrote a tutorial entitled "How to Read a Book".[74] In it, he explained his personal strategy for reading books, which was to search a book for information that was valuable and new, rather than reading it from cover to cover. His approach might involve going to the table of contents and finding an intriguing chapter, or thumbing through the book, skipping over what wasn't necessary. His point was simple: we are not obligated to read any book from cover to cover or even in a front-to-back direction.

This strategy also works for scientific articles. A colleague of mine who never had time for all of the journal articles that he wanted to read would make use of the time he had by just reading the abstract and the conclusion for an article, and making sure he understood the diagrams and graphs that the authors provided. This was his version of the approach that Bill Casey recommended to his analysts: a search-and-destroy mission rather than a thorough end-to-end vacuuming.

How to Find Good Books

One of the best ways to find good books is to ask others what they have read lately. When I was a program manager, for example, I would often use this question to open my meetings with contractors. After a few visits, they started to expect the question and were ready for me. It was like having an army searching for interesting books, and I got some great leads with that simple question.

A second way to find good books is to do the literary equivalent of a walkabout. One of my end-of-year rituals is roaming the stacks at a large Barnes and Noble store.[75] I wander through the nonfiction sections, pull books with interesting titles, look at the chapter headings, read about the author, and perhaps skim the introduction. If the book still seems interesting, I take a picture of it and put it on a list of potential reads for the year. Before I read any of the books on the list, I will do a more thorough review, using the questions described earlier. This guarantees that I always start the year with at least a few dozen books.

Finally, the reference section of any book can provide good leads to the next book. For example, I recently became interested in hydroponics. It seemed like a good way to improve my nutrition because it allowed me to grow some of my own leafy vegetables reliably and safely throughout the year. I started with a very simple how-to book, that left me with many questions. Fortunately, the reference section pointed me to a more detailed book, whose reference section finally pointed me to the book I really needed — one by a university professor who wasn't afraid of numbers. The last book was admittedly a tough read, but it gave me what I needed to understand the science behind my hydroponics.

The greatest value of a book is often the next book that it leads you to.

Some of the Best Insights Come From Good Fiction

A reading list should also include fiction that has survived time. Some of the enduring problems of humanity, for example, lie at the heart of many an allegory or novel. Need a few life lessons? Read some Ernest Hemingway or Harper Lee or Mary Shelley. Interested in moral character? Try Victor Hugo and Fyodor Dostoyevsky.

Fiction can also fuel our imagination as well as help us understand our humanity. Science fiction, for example, has inspired many technical researchers in the past and helped lead to devices as varied as submarines and helicopters (Jules Verne), rockets and atomic energy (H.G. Wells), robotic arms (Robert Heinlein), and mobile phones (Gene Rodenberry).[76]

The most dangerous form of fiction – and, unfortunately, also one of the most entertaining – is historical fiction. This genre employs plots that are imagined versions of past events and people. Fiction and nonfiction become entwined in this category, and the effect can play tricks with memory.

For example, I recently became trapped in this problem with a very entertaining book by Graham Moore entitled *The Last*

Days of Night.[77] The book concerned a patent battle between George Westinghouse and Thomas Edison over who was first to invent the electric light bulb. It came highly recommended by a friend and was named the best work of historical fiction of the year by the American Library Association. But after I read it, I could no longer trust myself with what I knew about Thomas Edison, George Westinghouse, and Nickola Tesla. I could not be sure if my recalled information was a figment of the *Last Days of Night* or a documented fact from one of the biographies that I had read earlier. As the author warns:

> *The Last Days of Night is a work of historical fiction. Apart from the well-known actual people, events, and locales that figure into the narrative, all names characters, places, and incidents are products of the author's imagination or are used fictitiously.*

There is not much we can do about this problem since it is rooted in how the brain remembers. We reconstruct memories from encoded information in various parts of the brain, rather than reading them off like video in RAM. As a result, we can sometimes recall a piece of information, but not necessarily where we read it.

The World Wide Web as a Source

There are few things in this world that have been as transformative as the internet and the world wide web. In seconds we can have answers to questions that used to take hours or days to find in an old-fashioned library.

Part of the problem with a gadzillion web pages is that within them, we can find any answer that we want to believe. So, how do we decide what is worth believing? The recipe (albeit imperfect) is straightforward: use the same questions that were discussed earlier for books, and apply the lessons of self-deception and deception by others to anything we want to take seriously from the internet. On popular issues such as politics, urban legends, myths, etc. sites like *Snopes* and *FactCheck* can sometimes help determine the validity of the things we discover, or at least provide a broader context for exploring the issue.[78]

It probably doesn't make much difference whether that goofy YouTube video of two guys vying for a Darwin Award is staged or true. But it does matter when deceptive news reports help elect a politician, or convince us to abandon our doctor's prescription and spend $59.95 for a miracle cure.

Getting to what you know and how you know it can be hard to do on the internet. Let's say, for example, that we are concerned about health and nutrition. No one has any trouble believing that a constant diet of fast food is bad. But after that, health and nutrition on the internet seems like a crap shoot. Don't eat dairy. Eat dairy. Don't eat beans. Eat beans. Don't eat tomatoes. Eat tomatoes. Don't take supplements. Take megadoses of supplements. Toxic cleansing is essential. Toxic cleanses are unnecessary. We can find arguments and theories that initially sound credible for either side. How do we figure any of this stuff out? And most importantly, how do we avoid doing something that might harm us?

My own preferences for web-based medical and nutritional information are research hospital sites like that of the Mayo

Clinic. Could they be biased on specific topics? Sure, but the likelihood that they are biased in a dangerous direction is far less than that for a randomly-chosen commercial businesses whose existence depends on a specific drug therapy or treatment. Are these highly-regarded-hospital sites a bit conservative? I hope so, since I am not interested in gambling my health as a guinea pig for an unproven idea.

I would not stop with a web site, however. I would also do exactly what I would do if there wasn't any internet to turn to. I would find sources who are credible, who study the evidence, and who understand the research. They would include dietitians, doctors, and university researchers.[79] I would ask them at least four questions:

- What does the preponderance of the best research say? How strong is the evidence and what are the major objections to the existing consensus?[80]
- What should my expectations be if I follow the recommendations?
- Are there any aspects of my particular health, lifestyle and age that would change these recommendations?
- What are the potential side effects or damage that might occur and how prevalent are they?

Asking such questions does not guarantee a completely satisfactory answer, of course. But posing good questions to knowledgeable people will rarely be a waste of time, no matter what the question at hand. Unlike exclusively using the web for answers, we can often get a perspective that relates more directly to us, and does not depend only on our interpretation of a web page that was written for a general audience.

We should keep two things foremost in our minds when surfing the web for information. First, we should not assume that everything we need to know can be found online using Google or Bing or Yahoo!. In fact, most of the content of the internet is hidden from these browsers in the so-called "deep web," which is on the order of 500 times the size of the surface web we use every day.[81] And second, we should not assume that everything we need to know can be found online on the first search results page that Google or any other search engine returns. A longstanding joke is that the best place to hide a dead body is on the second page of a Google search.

At the end of the day, we use the web at our own peril. A cautious mantra might be: *it's not all there and some of what is there is unproven, distorted or wrong*.

Astroturfing and Similar Internet Nonsense

Astroturfing is defined as "the practice of masking the sponsors of a message or organization to make it appear as though it originates from and is supported by grassroots participants."[82] It is a technique that hides the business and political connections behind a message, creating the impression that a base of support or common cause exists when it really doesn't.

Astroturfing long predates the internet, but it has really come into its own with the advent of social media. For example, Russian efforts to influence the 2016 presidential election used astroturfing and related methods to mislead voters. To do this, the perpetrators relied heavily on providers like Facebook and Twitter.

Supposedly, Facebook and some of the other providers have learned their lesson and are going to help keep this covert influence activity off of their sites. But this is an evolutionary game, and it would be foolish to assume that those companies will eliminate dangerously-deceptive influences.

Only we can fix this problem, by doing exactly what we should do with any information that feeds our decision processes – verify or discount it. Do not mindlessly pass it on. The Russians aren't paying us, but passing their propaganda on is the same as working for them. How does it feel to be in the same business as Robert Hanssen and Aldrich Ames?[83]

Part of a good strategy for avoiding internet disinformation is to tread lightly when we use internet sources to confirm other internet sources. To the extent possible, look for independent verification outside of the internet.[84] This is one reason that credible books and other well-informed sources need to remain high on our input list.

Media Reporting Biases

In general, television, newspapers, magazines, and internet media are not unbiased. While some sources are more liberal or conservative than others, and some are far more careful with reporting than others, all have different agendas that mirror the preferences of their owners and sponsors.

The most damaging bias in media reporting is the almost universal preference for the negative. This occurs because reporting bad news is far more profitable and conducive to high viewership than normal everyday goodness. Someone getting killed today in the U.S. always gets more attention than the fact that 350 million people did not get killed. Unfortunately, what isn't said – because it doesn't sell ads – is often far more insightful than what does.

In his book, *Factfulness: Ten Reasons We're Wrong About the World – and Why Things Are Better Than You Think*, Hans Rosling tries to debunk the wrong impressions that are created by overwhelmingly negative news reporting. Part of his effort is a website that hosts an insightful test to show us how well we really know the world.[85] The test includes multiple choice questions like: *How did the number of deaths per year from natural disasters change over the last hundred years*? and *How many people in the world have some access to electricity?* It essentially assesses the general impressions we have gained from watching countless tv news reports and news feeds.

When Rosling tested nearly 12,000 people in 14 countries in 2017, the average score was *two correct answers out of twelve questions*. Fifteen per cent of the test takers scored zero, an amazing result, given that choosing answers at random would have scored 4 out of 12. As Rosling notes, "There is no room for facts when our minds are occupied by fear."[86]

Another fundamental problem with the media is the fallacy of equal time. In a feature on climate change, for example, there is no compelling reason to give equal time to the conspiracy theorist who is sure that climate change is nothing but a government plot, and to the legitimate scientists who are studying climate change. Not all opinions are worth equal time, and such one-on-one faceoffs convey a false legitimacy to the fringe proponent. The amount of time or space allocated to a topic is not an indicator of its accuracy.

Can We Trust Pictures and Video?

Images are powerful tools of persuasion. Who for example, hasn't been motivated at some time or another to donate to a cause because of pictures or video of starving children, mistreated animals or natural disasters? Or outraged by a video of a terrorist shouting hateful messages or murdering a hostage? Or tempted to believe in the Loch Ness monster because, by golly, that fuzzy picture does sort of look like a Jurassic-era creature?

The recent explosion of cell phone video, go-pro cameras, security cameras, and traffic monitors is completely changing the way news is reported. Consider, for example, how much the dynamic between law enforcement and the public has changed as a result of the proliferation of compact video cameras and recorders. In many ways, images and movies are far more effective tools of persuasion than print or speech, and as a result, they will likely dominate much of the information that we get from the media.

Here are some things to remember when we see a picture or video designed to create an impression or motivate us to do something:

- Pictures and video are snapshots in time. We don't know what happened before or after. In magic, for example, tricks are often about what happened before the trick appeared to have started or after it ended.
- Pictures and video are snapshots in space. What was happening where the lens wasn't pointed? For example, is the local news report of damage due to some natural catastrophe typical of the overall damage in the area of impact, or is it simply the most damaged location that the reporter could find?
- Pictures and videos are taken from one vantage point. How does the scene look from other angles? A football play that appears to be a touchdown at one angle, for example, is sometimes a failed attempt when viewed from a different perspective.

Typically, a picture or video is selected to present or prove a specific interpretation that fits the media's message. We should always ask ourselves what that message is and whether alternative interpretations exist.

Beyond these basic caveats, there is the increasing possibility that pictures and video are deliberately manipulated or faked. Scammers and hoaxers have been faking photographs for more than 150 years, although the process was fairly complicated before digital photography and Photoshop ®. The first known fake was "Self-Portrait as a Drowned Man" done by Hippolyte Bayard to protest a controversy over whether he or Louis Daguerre should have been credited with inventing photography.[87] Since then, fake pictures have been used for everything from proving the existence of supernatural beings to discrediting political candidates, to selling cosmetics.

Like photographs, video can also be doctored to change a viewer's perspective on an issue. Some of these techniques include removing relevant portions of a longer tape, combining two or more different videos and presenting them as one event, substituting faces, and altering audio tracks.

In May of 2019, for example, the *Washington Post* reported that footage of a speech by House Speaker Nancy Pelosi had been altered to make her appear to slur her words.[88] While this fake was a fairly crude alteration of something that did occur, artificial intelligence will eventually allow instigators to create credible video of events that did not occur, including showing the President or some other public figure saying or doing something he or she did not do or say.[89] While technologies are being developed to detect such forgeries, this will likely become an evolutionary race between defense and offense. Hopefully, we won't be one of the mindless millions who simply forwards such unvalidated material to others.

Virtual Divisions

At one point in my life, I worked with a manager who had what I thought was the world's best job. He was the boss of an advanced concepts group in CIA's research office. I learned a lot from him, and especially the idea that it is always better to work with smart people than dumb people. It was his way of saying that we should hire the best, especially if they are smarter than we are. We shouldn't let our egos get in the way.

His advice also applies when we are seeking information from any type of source. Find the best and stick with them. Don't waste too much time with marginal sources or let ourselves be overly influenced by them. That means we go to the Mayo Clinic for serious medical information, not to an alternative medicine site. We use the ag extension office of our local university, not the guy at Lowes or Home Depot for gardening advice. We make our decisions on nutrition based on what our medical team suggests rather than what a vitamin ad on tv says.[90]

Essentially, we need to build a team of reliable and continuously-vetted sources. These include people, media, and other types of information and capabilities that can help us deliberate on whatever issue is on our mind, and provide access to others who might have the answers we need. [91]

But having access to good sources of information is not enough in and of itself. If we see the relationship between us and the "expert" as one in which he or she does all of the work and just tells us what to do and where to sign, then we are asking for trouble. On the other hand, if we view the relationship as one of respected partners, both (or many), contributing toward a reasonable solution, then we have a better chance of getting things right. An expert's purpose is not to tell us what to do, but rather to work with us to find solutions.[92]

In an earlier book dealing with program management in government, Bruce Hartmann and I described such a group of reliable sources as a virtual division.[93] In our example, the virtual division was all of our trusted operations people and contractors and consultants and enablers and funders that we needed to run programs and deliver products. These were not necessarily people in the same office sitting at the desks next to us or down the hall. Our team was scattered throughout the entire organization, the government, the country, and the world.

As an example, Figure 5 shows what a personal virtual division might look like for some of life's more important health decisions.

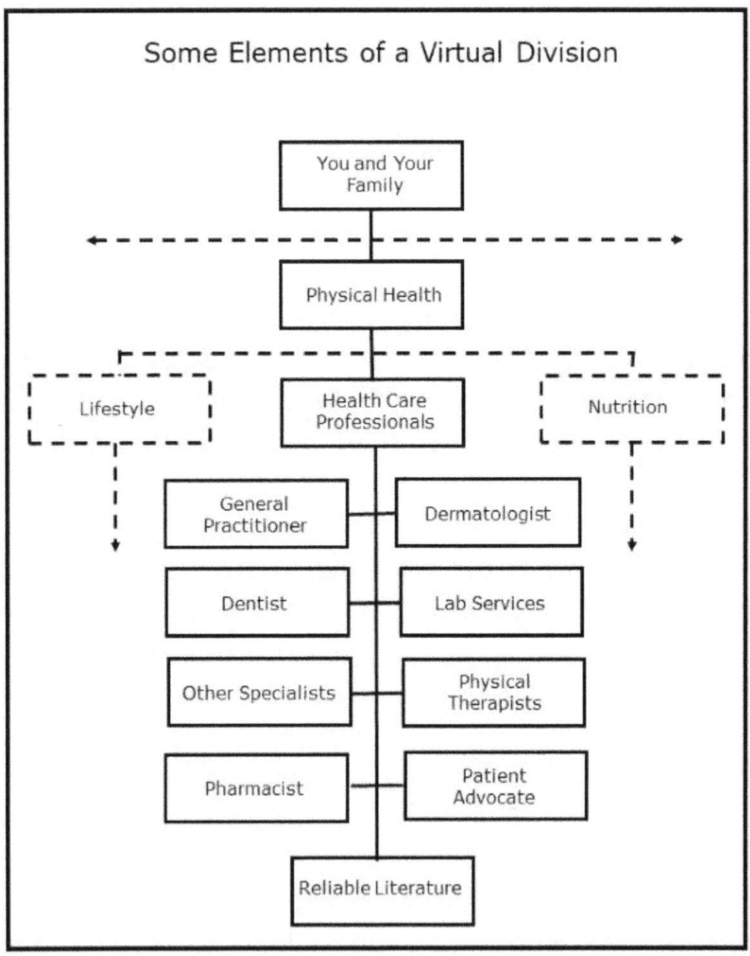

Figure 5. Some Elements of a Virtual Division

I've structured this like a business organization because in a sense that is what it represents – our resources to run our lives. While most of the blocks represent people with real expertise and experience, the example also includes a block called reliable literature. This is all of the books, magazines web sites, blogs, TED talks, etc. that we have found reliable, understandable, and relevant. Often, they will be the source of insights that become topics of discussions and strategy to use with others in the division.

In my case, for example, the reliable literature block under the Health Care Professionals segment contains hospital web sites like m*ayoclinic.org* and journals like *The New England Journal of Medicine.* It also contains books I've found helpful on topics like medical statistics, how to read medical articles, and how doctors think. It even includes those printed instructions that come with any medications I am currently taking.

My reliable literature block also includes references that are highly critical of the health professions. The science and technology of health is a work in progress and does not get everything right. For example, the profession is being highly criticized by some today for over prescribing tests and overmedicating patients.[94] Understanding controversial issues like this can help us to better question what a particular doctor recommends or asks us to consider.

So, what does your virtual division look like for the challenges you face? Are you surrounded by resources that give you the accurate and reliable information and insight you need to ask better questions and make better decisions? Or, do you just depend on whatever the first page of a Google search throws at you?

Finally, these organizational diagrams (be they health related, finance related, property related, or capture some other decision-making process you care about) show the existence of relationships, but — as suggested earlier — they do not capture the nature of those relationships. A virtual division only works to the extent that the interactions are two-way, well-informed and well cared for.

To make a virtual division effective, you have to work hard with your team to understand the problem that it is helping to resolve. For example, don't take a car to a shop mechanic without some idea of what the problem is, including a well-thought-out list of the symptoms and when they occur. Don't visit an investment advisor without a prior estimate of financial status and goals. Don't go to a doctor without accurately documenting symptoms and preparing a list of questions in advance. In other words, try to be an equal and well-prepared partner in these relationships, rather than just the person who writes the checks.

It's Our Choice

The good news is that we all get to choose what we want to use as input for our decisions and opinions. But along with that right should come a responsibility to make sure that those sources are as accurate as possible. Otherwise, we are simply contributing to the background noise that does no one any good.

CHAPTER FOUR

Believing Science, but Not Scientists

What you know about science is more important than the science you know – Harry Collins and Trevor Pinch

The problems we face today as individuals and societies increasingly have a scientific component. Are vaccines safe? Is the climate really changing because of us? Is the food we eat harmful? We look to science for reliable answers to such questions. Yet as a public, we know and understand relatively little about the scientific professions that try to provide answers. That ignorance doesn't keep us from having strong opinions, however. Try, for example, putting a public health scientist in the same room with any of the nearly 1-in-10 Americans who believe that vaccines are not safe.[95]

Some believe that Americans should know more science. We need more biology, more physics, and more chemistry in our schools. As if it is our fault, for example, that we don't understand the complex positive and negative feedback loops that determine the effects of climate change. Or what really constitutes "safe enough" in the food we eat, the water we drink, and the air we breathe. Clearly, education *is* necessary. But instead of trying to understand the scientific details behind each and every important issue, perhaps we need to work a bit on the far more accessible task of understanding the limits of science in general, the limits of what we are likely to really understand as laypersons, and the important difference between what a scientist has reported and scientific consensus.[96]

Afterall, which should matter more in a personal decision: the ability to parrot a few scientific terms, or an understanding of the strengths and limitations of the process that led to a particular scientific finding?

Scientific Expertise

How much science do most of us really know? To answer the question, it might help to think of scientific expertise in terms of these four categories:

- Those who are well grounded in science and are capable of original work in their field. They are practicing scientists.
- Those who understand a scientific field and its challenges, methods, and language, but are not active

in the field. They might be former practicing scientists or simply nonscientists who are passionate about a particular issue. They know and understand the literature and the key players, and go far beyond popular books on a subject.

- Those who read popular books on a scientific topic, but are somewhat lost in the field's language and methods. They may sound good when they talk about a problem, but their knowledge is often superficial.
- Those whose understanding of a particular field is almost nonexistent. Much of the information that they get on the science of an issue is the passing 3-minute segment on the news or a web page. They know a few science words, but would struggle to define them.

Almost all of us fall into the last two categories on most scientific fields. And we always will. No one can reasonably expect the average person to understand the issues and limitations of the wide range of scientific concerns that we face.

Dissecting a Scientific Experiment

Science is built largely on the idea of using experiments to test hypotheses. In their book, *The Golem*, British sociologists Harry Collins and Trevor Pinch describe an experiment in which students discover the boiling point of water by heating a beaker of water to boiling and observing the resulting temperature.[97] In many ways, this basic experiment provides a straightforward way of illustrating how science works, how easily any scientist can be wrong, and how science achieves consensus.

A more modern version of the experiment they described almost 30 years ago might look like this. Six students from around the U.S. are participating in an online science course that includes an experiment to determine the boiling point of water. The teacher provides some very general guidance for the assignment, but each student runs the experiment alone. They report the following results:

- Student 1: 101 degrees
- Student 2: 98 degrees
- Student 3: 212 degrees
- Student 4: 94 degrees
- Student 5: 99 degrees
- Student 6: 100 degrees

After the experiment is over, the teacher and the students get together to discuss the results and carefully review their procedures. In the end, they agree on a result (100 degrees), and uncover some of the complications underlying this seemingly simple experiment.

- Student 1 reported 101 degrees. A review of this student's effort revealed that she did not understand that the water had to be pure and used a dirty beaker in her experiment. As a result, her water was contaminated with salt that raised its boiling point. Later experiments would show that the increase in boiling point depends on the concentration of the contaminant in the water, but not its composition.

- Student 2: reported 98 degrees. When this student's work was reexamined, it was found that his thermometer was incorrectly calibrated. This was corrected by new lab procedures that required recalibration of lab instruments before any measurements were taken.
- Student 3 reported 212 degrees. The procedure was correct in this case, but the answer was reported in different units —Fahrenheit instead of Celsius. (If you think this never happens in science, note that NASA likely lost a $125 million Mars orbiter in 1999 because of English-Metric unit confusion.)[98]
- Student 4 reported 94 degrees. In his case, he worked online from home in Colorado, at an altitude that was 5000 feet higher than where the other experiments took place. Since water boils at lower temperatures when the atmospheric pressure is reduced, his number was lower than those obtained at sea level. Later lab work by the students quantified the relationship between pressure and boiling point.
- Student 5 reported 99 degrees. After some discussion, he revealed that he did not stir the water continuously and probably made the measurement before all of the water in the beaker was at the boiling point.
- Student 6 reported 100 degrees. A review of her work showed that it was done with care, that the equipment was properly calibrated, that water was pure and that the atmospheric pressure was 14.7 psi. After some additional laboratory investigations, the group agreed that this was likely the correct answer for the measured pressure.

Although this is a simplistic example, it does illustrate that many issues occur in science experiments, including variations in methods, misinterpretations of procedure, lack of control of conditions, misunderstandings, variation in location, and other factors that few recognize initially. These complications lead to different results and different conclusions, and sometimes suggest new paths for investigation.

The most important part of the student exercise was not the individual experiments, but rather the information sharing and discussion that occurred afterward. This exchange revealed deficiencies in some the work as well as factors that hadn't been considered initially. Scientists refer to this latter stage as peer review.

In the scientific world, peer review usually starts after the research is done and the paper is submitted to a journal for publication review. Journal editors select knowledgeable scientists to read and consider the quality of the article, including the procedures used by the authors, how they analyzed the data and how they interpreted the results. Based on those comments, the editors decide whether the paper should be accepted for publication, revised by the authors and published later, or rejected.[99]

Formal peer review has not always been part of science and it is evolving with the times. The practice started in the 1700s, but did not become the norm until the mid-twentieth century.[100] Today, with the availability of the internet and world wide web, the process is becoming more open. Some journals, for example, publish the formal peer reviews and use their websites for further comment and review.[101]

In a sense, the publication review process is only the beginning of peer review, as published papers are then read and considered by the journal's readers. Even with the many eyes of a journal's readership on a published paper, however, errors (and even scientific fraud) can sometimes be difficult to detect.

Scientific Error and Bias

As the boiling water experiment showed, identifying sources of error and bias is fundamental to science. Good scientists carefully calibrate their instruments, select representative samples or subjects to investigate, completely define and rigidly follow protocols, control conditions, correctly analyze their results, limit their conclusions to what the data support, and subject their results to peer review.

And despite all of that effort, it is often insufficient to ensure reliable results. Published results often cannot be replicated or confirmed by other researchers.[102]

Not all of the blame can be placed on the shoulders of individual scientists, however. Some biases are endemic to science itself.

When scientists report a statistically significant result, this means that there is some low probability (say, 5% or less) that their conclusion is wrong. In other words, they might be reporting that an effect exists when it really doesn't, simply because of chance. This often happens when a sample used in a research study does not actually represent its population as a whole. When this occurs, the estimate of the mean and variability of the population that are obtained from the sample will not reflect the true values of the population. A study to determine the average weight of men in the U.S., for example, would be misleading if by chance all of its data happened to come from men who played in the National Football League.

A 5% chance of being wrong doesn't sound too bad at first glance. But, add to that a bias for publishing positive results and we are in dangerous waters. The danger is especially high in scientific fields in which there are numerous possible relationships to test and few that have true cause-and-effect relationships. An example is the tens of thousands of genes in the human genome and how each of them (alone or in some combination) might or might not contribute to a specific disease. A huge number of possible relationships exist, but only a few will be meaningful.[103]

When scientists test these potential cause-and-effect relationships, they will discover one of four possibilities:

- a relationship when there actually is one (a true positive),
- a relationship when there isn't one (a false positive),
- no relationship when there is one (a false negative), or
- no relationship when there isn't one (a true negative).

Each option has a different probability of occurring, but the first two will both be considered positive results.

Because of a bias toward publishing positive results, scientists will selectively report the true relationships that they find *and* the false relationships that turned out positive by chance alone. When there are lots of opportunities for false positives and relatively few actual positives, then most of the reported results will be wrong.[104] This is, in part, why many of the promising preliminary results that are reported in the literature turn out to be false alarms.

The essential flaw is that decisions are being made on the results of individual studies rather than the totality of the evidence. Negative results are far *less* likely to be published than positive results. Physicist Richard Feynman pointed this out almost 50 years ago, yet scientists and publishers still succumb to it.[105] The effect is a bit like the media's preference for negative news.

Science Can Change Its Mind

People sometimes get upset when they are told that scientific facts are temporary, but that is because they confuse what is believed at the time with absolute truth.[106] We don't know what we don't know. Consequently, it is a gray world, not a black and white world.

Isaac Asimov referred to this effect as *the relativity of wrong* in his classic essay of the same title.[107] Using the example of the earth's shape, he explained how at one time, we thought the world was flat. Later, early scientists figured out that it was a sphere, and this was eventually proven true in multiple ways. Once the sphere model was accepted, scientists later showed that the earth is slightly compressed at the poles and bulging at the equator, a shape that is sometimes referred to as an oblate spheroid. More recently, experiments have shown that the earth also bulges slightly below the equator. In other words, it is also a tiny bit pear-shaped. So, the "facts" about the earth's shape changed with additional knowledge and instrumentation, but the relativity of their wrongness decreased. Scientists didn't jump from a plate to a sphere to a cube, but rather from a plate to a sphere to a slightly-less-than spherical object.

We see these shifts in understanding frequently. In 1998, for example, the National Institutes of Health changed its definitions of obesity, and overnight 25 million Americans suddenly became fat. Under the old guidelines, a person who was 5 feet, 10 inches tall and weighed 185 pounds was considered overweight. Under the new guidelines, a person of the same height was now overweight at 175 pounds.[108] The guidelines were changed because new research and analyses showed a somewhat stronger linkage than previously thought between body fat and serious health problems such as heart disease. The scientific consensus changed somewhat. In a sense, obesity guidelines went from a sphere to a slightly less than spherical object.

Sometimes, scientific facts change because they were never really scientific facts to begin with. Occasionally, preliminary scientific ideas are transformed into scientific fact, not by science, but by politicians, advocates, overly-zealous scientists, and the media.

One of the best examples of this effect is probably the U.S. obsession with low-fat diets that has lasted for several generations. This obsession was initially based on weak scientific evidence and very strong advocacy. Nevertheless, official dietary guidelines were developed based on this insufficient data, and the evidence that policies and recommendations might be wrong was ignored.[109]

Today, we have a better understanding of complex issues like saturated and unsaturated fats and good and bad cholesterol.[110] Looking back, we can see the Asimov progression in the following very brief history of diet/heart health.

Early studies of diet and heart health. In the early part of the 20th century, the most prominent causes of death in the U.S. were pneumonia and influenza, tuberculosis, and gastrointestinal infections. Once deaths from these infectious diseases declined, however, the population started living longer and dying from heart disease became more common.[111] In 1900, heart disease was only the fourth leading cause of death, but by the 1920s it had become the leading cause of death.[112]

By studying the incidence of heart disease in different populations around the world, scientists developed a hypothesis that the amount of fat consumed was related to the incidence of cardiovascular disease. Specifically, dietary fat led to high serum cholesterol levels in the blood, that in turn led to hardening of the arteries and heart attacks. Later, those ideas were refined to focus on saturated fats and distinct blood lipids like LDL, HDL and triglycerides.

Eventually, the government, the American Heart Association and others with a strong belief in the low-fat hypothesis began to issue "heart healthy" dietary guidelines. These included eating less fat, substituting unsaturated fats for saturated fats, and avoiding foods high in cholesterol. Some scientists objected to these guidelines at the time because they were not strongly supported by scientific evidence. Nonetheless, many

Americans and the food industry got caught up in a low-fat frenzy that lasted for decades.

Diet/heart health today. Scientists now understand that the original hypothesis and solution was simplistic at best, and missed many important details. In a recent article in the *British Medical Journal*, Nita Forouhi and her research colleagues summarized the history and evidence for dietary fat and heart health.[113] Here are several of their conclusions emphasizing how our understanding has changed. They are verbatim. Note the caution of the wording (The comments that follow are mine, and added for clarification).

- *For cardiovascular health, substantial evidence supports the importance of the type of fat consumed, not total fat intake, and the elimination of industrially produced trans fats.* Total fat consumed is probably not the problem it was originally thought to be, although studies still conflict over this overarching question. On the other hand, one very common unsaturated fat (trans) is very bad for our health.
- *Much of the evidence suggests that the risk of coronary heart disease is reduced by replacing saturated fat with polyunsaturated fats (including plant oils) but not when carbohydrate is the replacement nutrient.* Some fats are essential, such as the omega-3 fatty acids that come from some plants and fish. Our bodies do not make them, so we have to eat them. We also understand that simply replacing saturated fats with carbohydrate (like simple sugars) does not help heart problems.
- *The focus of dietary advice must be on the consumption of foods and overall dietary patterns,*

> *not on single nutrients.* This last conclusion is particularly interesting because it is a shift in how we often think about diet and health research. The focus on a specific nutrient (fat, protein, and carbohydrate) might not be the right way to think about the problem of diet and disease. For example, *saturated fat* is somewhat meaningless since the health effects of different foods with high levels of saturated fat are different. While a food might contain saturated fats, it might also contain other components that are really good for us.[114]

Someone who distains science might argue that these conclusions show that science has no idea what it is doing. Look, for example, how these scientists are changing their philosophy and advice on how they view nutrients! Doesn't that suggest that they are just full of themselves? Not really. Science moves in the direction that the data and analyses take it, and sometimes that leads to big changes in thinking. I might be tempted to argue that in the case of heart disease and diet, we are somewhere between a flat plate and a sphere rather than between a sphere and an oblate spheroid.

There are still many open questions on the complex subject of diet and heart disease, and not everyone agrees with the above view. But anyone who tries to turn this issue into simple yes/no answers today is over reaching. The grim reality is that good science on nutrition and long-term health effects is just not that easy to do. One challenge, for example, is obtaining accurate data on dietary intake. No objective observer is watching someone over a 20-or 30-year period, writing down everything they eat or drink. Much of what passes for data in this field is self-reported, with all of the biases and inaccuracies that implies.

There Is a Difference Between Science and Scientists

As the earlier examples suggest, what science says and what a scientist says are not necessarily the same thing. One is what an individual believes and the other is a high degree of consensus of scientists as a group. On average, better decisions lie collective judgement.

Scientists always have their own motivations, biases and limitations in what they promote. What should matter in our own decision making, therefore, is less what an individual scientist thinks and more what the scientific community concludes.

Ideas become more widely accepted in science as evidence for them builds, and they become less accepted as evidence piles up against them. Eventually a scientific consensus is reached, as it has, for example, in regard to climate change and its man-made origins. The first paper to estimate the contribution of carbon dioxide to the greenhouse effect was published in 1896 by Swedish scientist Savante Arrhenius.[115] While he did not go so far as to suggest that burning fossil fuels would cause future global warming. he did estimate its contribution at the time to atmospheric CO2. Thousands of research papers and 120+ years later, we have a very high degree of consensus that climate change is largely caused by human activity and — in the absence of change — the impact will be grim for many in the world.[116]

Scientists argue long and hard for their positions, and that debate is critical to scientific progress. What is often blamed by critics as resistance to new ideas is simply skepticism by those who know the complexities of any issue. But there are always dissenters, particularly among those who have a hard time letting go when their idea is discredited. An old science joke, for example, is that theories die only when those who proposed them die.

Unfortunately, not all of this debate is done in the interest of truth. In *Merchants of Doubt*, for example, authors Naomi Oreskes and Erik Conway describe efforts by some scientists and manufacturers to cloud scientific issues such as cigarettes and lung cancer. The strategy used by these obstructionists was to create the impression that significant scientific doubt still existed about an issue, and to use that doubt to delay government regulation that might adversely affect profits.[117]

In today's climate change debate, one can see the effects of similar efforts to repudiate the strong consensus that exists among climate scientists. While the scientific consensus for anthropogenic global warming is very high among knowledgeable scientists, the general public still maintains the impression that the consensus is weak. Those who are most dismissive of climate change believe that the consensus among climate scientists is less than half what it really is (44%, versus 97%).[118]

The tactics used to bamboozle the public and prevent climate change legislation are similar to those used in the lung cancer/smoking debates: spread doubt about scientific results in order to undermine the public view of scientific consensus. As long as the scientific consensus is in serious doubt, there is no compelling reason for government to act. Scientists can try to fight such tactics, but deniers have a large bag of tricks. These include cognitive biases such as cherry picking discredited articles that support their point of view, taking statements by climate scientists out of context, employing experts with questionable credentials, using logical fallacies liberally, and occasionally playing the conspiracy card.[119]

Some Things to Look for in Scientific Studies

Most of us get scientific news from the general news media, but that should always be taken with a grain of salt. Some sources are better than others. National Public Radio's *Science Friday*, The Society for Science and The Public's *Science News,* Springer Nature's *Scientific American,* and MIT's *Technology Review,* as well as websites like *Nature News,* are usually more reliable sources for general information. If we want to venture past these popular science descriptions and into the scientific literature itself, here are some of the things that we should look for or ask about in deciding whether the work has merit.

The type of study. There are many different types of research studies that address problems we face as individuals, such as good nutrition, effective medical treatment, and dependable finances. An important general distinction among these studies is whether the work is experimental or observational. In an experimental study, a variable is manipulated while other factors are controlled. For example, a drug study might involve people who are randomly assigned to a group that gets a treatment (the drug under investigation) and one that gets a placebo (the sugar pill). The assumption underlying such tests is that on average the two groups will be identical except for the treatment. If the results of the two groups are significantly different, we conclude that the difference was due to the treatment. In observational studies, on the other hand, researchers do not have the same level of control. Instead, they might look at a relationship or correlation that exists naturally among variables in a population under study. For example, one might compare the incidence of disease among people who have led active or sedentary lives or the incidence of lung cancer among smokers and nonsmokers.

While experimental results can prove direct cause and effect, observational studies provide a weaker form of evidence. In general, relationships found in observational studies are more likely to be considered causal if a dose-response relationship is found (heavy smokers are more likely to have lung cancer than light smokers) or if there is a plausible cause/effect theory for the relationship (many of the components of cigarette smoke are known carcinogens). Despite this limitation, observational studies are sometimes the only practical option. If we want to understand the relationship between childhood exposure to radiation and its effect on long-term health, for example, creating a treatment group (children who were deliberately exposed to known quantities and types of radiation) would be unethical.[120]

The size of the study and the magnitude of the effect. Whether a particular study can successfully find an effect or not depends largely on the size of the study and the magnitude of the effect. Scientists use the term "power" to describe the *probability* that a study can actually find the effect it is looking for. A study with low power has little chance of finding the effect while a study with high power has a greater chance.

Say, for example, we wanted to do an experiment to determine if a coin is unbalanced. If the coin is highly unbalanced, it would only take a few tosses to figure this out. If we tossed it 10 times and got only tails (which has a probability of 1 in 1024), we'd probably be confident that the coin was not evenly balanced. On the other hand, if we tossed a coin that was only slightly unbalanced the same number of times, we probably wouldn't be sure if it was biased. If ten tosses yielded tails 6 times, for example, would we really be sure of the coin? In this second case, our sample size (the number of times we flipped the coin) would need to be much larger in order to be confident in our answer.[121] To have the same power, each case would require a different sample size.

It is a sad fact that many scientific studies are underpowered, and the chances of error are greatest when both the sample size and the effect to be detected are small.[122] One has to wonder why a scientist would do such studies, but it can be an effective career strategy in a publish-or-perish world.[123]

Sometimes, many similar studies are analyzed as a group as way to increase the statistical power. Such statistical studies are known as meta-analyses, and are often a better source of information than single studies.[124]

The rigor of the experiment. Good experiments are very carefully designed and executed to reduce bias and avoid confounding factors. This includes taking great care to ensure that the control and treatment groups are identical. Since experimenter bias is also possible, many experiments are run with the researcher and study participants unaware of which subjects were given the real treatment. A weak study, on the other hand, does a poor job selecting treatment and control groups and does little to avoid investigator bias. One can often get a feel for the rigor of the experiment by how well the authors address potential pitfalls in their procedures and analysis.

The journal it is published in. To minimize time spent on poor work, look for well-respected journals, and especially those with a high impact factor.[125] Avoid fringe publications and predatory journals where almost anything can get published if the money is there. Some university library websites can provide excellent guidance for identifying legitimate and predatory journals.[126] Also be cautious when scientists bypass the peer review process and go directly to the press.[127]

The clarity of the end point. A test result can be objective, like a measurement of someone's height or weight, or subjective, like a statement of the level of pain they feel. In the latter case, results are going to be more susceptible to influence and individual interpretation.

The conflicts of interest. As noted earlier, be aware of potential conflicts of interest, both by the authors and the sponsors. Of course, just because a potential conflict of interest exists, does not necessarily mean that the results were influenced. Conflicts of interest are simply a caution flag.[128]

Replication. As we saw earlier, a study can sometimes produce a positive result when none really exists. But a study that has been replicated (that is, successfully repeated by other scientists) has a far greater chance of being correct. Always ask if others have confirmed the results by independently reproducing the experiment.

What other knowledgeable scientists are saying. Sometimes, other scientists will comment on the study in a letters-to-the-editor section or in online commentary. Authors of related articles can also provide indicators of their belief in the work, such as by citing it as a reference in their own papers.

The quality of the references. How well a paper is referenced can be an indication of its quality. In judging papers, we should always move beyond the paper itself, and consider the references that the authors used. For example, have they authors considered all relevant prior work? Are the bulk of the references their own or do they recognize relevant work done by others? Are the references credible, or is the paper based on implausible prior work?

In considering these 9 factors, we are ultimately trying to answer three questions about a given issue:

- What do most scientists agree is true?
- Why do they believe it?
- How strong are the legitimate arguments against it?

These are *what do I know and how do I know it?* questions. We are looking for these answers not because they guarantee correctness, but because they are based on the best-available and best-scrutinized knowledge. And, perhaps most importantly, they are the product of a process that will revise its answers if sufficient data becomes available that shows some aspect of the consensus is wrong.

If we can answer questions like these three with any depth, we probably know quite a bit about an issue. If we can't answer them, on the other hand, then what we know is probably superficial and not necessarily something we want to count on.

Science is Not Easy

The novelist Margaret Atwood once noted that "science is a tool, and we invent tools to do things we want. It is a question of how those tools are used by people."[129] While she meant this comment in the context of what science investigates, it can also apply to us as laymen who must deal with the results that science produces. Knowing the strengths and weaknesses of the process that produces scientific results, how do we use them in our decision making? Becoming truly knowledgeable about science and scientific issues is challenging, and this is in part why the virtual division concept discussed in Chapter 3 matters. A basic understanding of the strengths and weaknesses of science can help us to formulate good questions for our team. In decision making (and science), knowing the right question to ask is often the key.

CHAPTER FIVE

How Numbers Help and Harm Decisions

...knowing that it takes only about eleven and a half days for a million seconds to tick away, whereas almost thirty-two years are required for a billion seconds to pass, gives one a better grasp of the relative magnitudes of these two common numbers — John Allen Paulos

It is no secret that Americans as a whole are poor at math. Paulos coined the term "innumeracy" to refer to our general inability to cope "comfortably with numbers, probabilities, logic, and other basic notions of math." [130] One of his biggest gripes was that many Americans seemed proud of their inability to deal with the subject.[131]

I blame some of my college teachers for my own discomfort with many types of math. While I loved math as an adolescent and took as many math courses as I could in school, I eventually reached a point where none of it made much sense anymore. I distinctly remember the day that I was hopelessly stuck on some obscure theorem and decided that I was done. I never took another math course after that. From then on, I depended on engineering courses to teach me the math that I needed to know. For me — and I suspect for many others — math is only interesting when it can be used to solve an immediate practical problem.

While most accept the prevalence of innumeracy, there is less agreement on just how mathematically literate the average American should be. The good news is that we probably don't need to know as much as our school teachers led us to believe. Chances are that no one will ever ask us to prove the Pythagorean Theorem or find the surface area of a sphere using integration.[132]

On the other hand, a few basic arithmetic and mathematical skills can mean a big difference when making decisions. For me, the top three are:

- A sense of what numbers and units mean. As Paulos suggests, it helps to have some handle on the difference between a million and a billion.
- An ability to do simple algebraic calculations, understand simple relationships between variables, and interpret graphs.
- An appreciation for probability and how to deal with misleading terms like *percent* and *average*.

There is also a fourth basic skill — doing back-of-the-envelope calculations. But it is not for everyone. Even people who are good at math can be lousy at this last skill because it requires an ability to estimate the value of unknowns. I've included a short tutorial as the last section in this chapter for those who are curious about the technique.

Learning to Think More Quantitatively

We are far better at asking ourselves whether something is or isn't than asking ourselves *how much* something is or isn't. *How much* allows us to better understand shades of gray, not just black and white. And that can lead to better results.

Many nutritional decisions, for example, are fundamentally quantitative, yet few treat them as such. How many times have we heard that organic foods are good for us? Or that GMOs are bad? These statements sound good. They sound knowledgeable. Unfortunately, they are largely meaningless. Just how good or how bad or how much or how little is what really matters when it comes to what we know and how we know it.

In this example, our decisions matter not only because they affect our nutritional health, but also because we incur opportunity costs. At first blush, one might say that food decisions should be based on health not dollars. But those dollars we spend on organic food, for example, could be used instead to improve all sorts of life's health problems, many of which could be more consequential than whether or not we eat organically. Getting our dental problems addressed, buying new glasses, living in a safer neighborhood, buying a more reliable car, getting a checkup, and fixing that nagging cough might each yield a far better payoff.

Knowing how much we benefit or are harmed by doing or not doing something should play a far bigger role in our decisions than it typically does.

Improving Our Feel for Numbers

We have all at one time or another looked at a number and wondered *what the heck does that mean*? Most of us have problems relating to numbers, particularly when they are very large or very small.

Scientists who communicate effectively often use analogy to put numbers into a clearer context. Jason Wright, an astronomy professor at Penn State University, provides a nice example. His work involves trying to answer the age-old question of whether we are alone in the universe by searching the heavens for other planets that might hold life.

In a recent paper, Wright made the point that we have only searched a tiny fraction of possible space. But instead of just citing a figure, he compared space to the earth's oceans and noted that volume so far investigated is equivalent to a very large hot tub. Clearly anyone, and especially non-scientists, reading his answer will have a better appreciation of the problem than had he simply noted the fraction of space that has been searched: roughly 1/170,000,000,000,000,000.[133] The visual image that he conveyed is far more insightful than citing a tiny fraction.

We can do the same sort of thing with numbers we encounter as a way of gaining a new understanding or perspective. Simply ask what that obscure amount means in terms that we can better relate to.

For example, let's say we are interested in buying a new car to commute to work. We really like the big Ford SUV and can purchase it on time with $500 monthly payments for 7 years. The total loan cost is $42,000, and we think we can handle that. But instead of just going with our gut, we do a simple calculation. How long would we have to work to pay the loan off? Since we make $30 an hour, and take home $20 after taxes, insurance, retirement, etc., we would need to work for an entire year *with no other expenses* to pay it off. Since there are 2,080 work hours in a normal year:

Time to pay off = $42,000 / ($20/hour * 2080/year)
Time to pay off =1.01 year

In this new context, that cheaper SUV in the used car lot might be a saner option. Or perhaps that car mechanics course at the local community college is an even better alternative.[134]

Heuristics and Simple Calculations

We often use heuristics or rules of thumb to avoid doing a bit of arithmetic.[135] In compound interest calculations, for example, one popular heuristic is the rule of 72. This rule states that the amount of time required to double our money equals 72 divided by our rate of return. If we invest money at a 10 percent annual return, we will double our money every

7.2 years. (72/10 = 7.2). If we invest our money at only 2 percent, it will double in 36 years.

While the rule of 72 can be useful for some types of questions, understanding its basis lets us answer many other types of financial questions. This particular heuristic is based on the yearly compound interest formula:

Amount at time, t = Principal * (1 + interest rate)^t

Where t is typically the time in years, the annual interest rate is expressed as a decimal (5% is 0.05 and 50% is 0.5, for example) and the principal is the amount originally invested.

Since the rule is limited to the case where the principal doubles, the ratio of amount to principal is fixed at 2:

Amount/Principal = (1 + interest rate)^t = 2

As noted earlier, the rule of 72 predicts 7.2 years for an interest rate of 10% (72/10). But how do we get this same result from the compound interest formula? To do that, we have to solve the equation for time, or t.

The challenge, of course, is that t is an exponent and it takes a bit of trickery (logarithms) to solve the equation.[136] Solving the equation for t starts by taking the logarithm of both sides:

Log 2 = t * log (1 + 0.1);
t= log 2 / log 1.1
t = (0.301) / (0.0414) = 7.27 years

While the math might look abstract at first glance, this is what the Log and y ^ x functions do on the scientific calculator in our cell phones.[137]

Why go to such trouble? While the equation is far harder than the rule of 72, it is also far more useful. It can answer questions that the rule of thumb can't. For example:

- How much that 19.24% credit card interest is going to set us back.
- How much an early withdrawal from our IRA will cost us in the end.
- Whether the end-of-life insurance that is often hawked on television is right for us.
- How much that storage locker that we have had for 5 years has cost us.

A little effort on a basic formula can often be far more useful than a handful of heuristics.[138]

Exponential Growth

The compound interest formula has a wide range of decision-making applications beyond interest rates and finances because it unveils the more general concept of exponential growth. We had a quick peek at this in Chapter 1, with the third question in the intuition-versus-deliberation test:

> *In a lake, there is a patch of lily pads. Every day, the patch doubles in size. If it takes 48 days for the patch*

to cover the entire lake, how long would it take for the patch to cover half of the lake?

Exponential growth occurs when the rate of growth is proportional to the amount that exists, such as the lily pad patch doubling in size every day. It takes 47 days to cover the first half of the lake and only one more day to cover the entire lake. This doubling effect is like compound interest when the time period is a day and the interest rate is 100% or 1:

full coverage/half coverage= 2 = (1 + growth rate)^t

=2 = (1 + 1)^t

2=2^t

t=1

There is an old story about the invention of the game of chess that dramatically illustrates the power of exponential growth. The inventor showed his new game to the ruler of India who was so delighted that he asked the inventor to name his own reward. The inventor responded by asking for one grain of rice for the first square on the chess board, two for the second square, 4 for the third square, and so on through the 64th square. This sounded like a very modest award, so the ruler agreed to it.

He should have done the math, however. It goes like this: There are sixty-four squares on the chessboard. One grain of rice is on the first square. Two grains of rice are on the second square. Four grains on the third square. By the 64th day, the number of grains of rice on the last square on the chessboard are:

Number of grains = (1+interest rate)^63;

where the interest rate is 100% or 1 (doubling the amount on the previous square is an interest rate of 100%). Continuing:

Number of grains = (1+1)^63 = 2^63;

or 9,223,000,000,000,000,000!

A bit of arithmetic and an estimate for the weight of one grain of rice (29 mg) will show that total weight of the rice on the last square is in the range of 300,000,000,000 tons. For perspective, the total weight of all human beings on the earth is only 316,000,000 tons or about 1000 times less.[139]

Why should exponential growth and a story about chess matter to us? Many of the problems that the world faces today such as the instabilities of climate change, the spreading of disease, the growth of populations, and even technological progress, can proceed exponentially rather than linearly. If we always think linearly — things will increase or decrease at the same pace they are now — we misjudge the seriousness of many problems and the benefits of many opportunities. And that won't lead to better decisions.[140]

Beware of Graphs

Charles Munger, Vice-Chairman of Berkshire Hathaway and Warren Buffett's business partner, once said that "mankind invented a system to cope with the fact that we are so intrinsically lousy at manipulating numbers. It's called the graph."[141]

As Munger notes, graphs can make many things clearer, but when someone sticks a graph in our faces in order to prove a point or help us make a decision, we should pay very close attention.

The subtleties of graphs and charts and the ways in which they can mislead us would fill an entire book. Here are a few of the more common issues that everyone should know about these tools.

- The starting point of an axis is not always zero.
- Graphs sometimes use axes that are not linear.
- Those who create graphs sometimes omit important data.
- Graphs are not, in and of themselves, good predictors of the future.

Each is a potential pitfall that can cause us to misinterpret information and make wrong decisions.

The Starting Point of an Axis. The vertical and horizontal axes on a graph do not have to start at zero. Sometimes, this is simply a practicality. There is no reason, for example, that a graph showing yearly trends in the 20th century need start at 0 CE. On the other hand, departures from zero can make quite a difference in how we perceive trends. Consider the following figure that shows the average (January-December) surface temperature of the United States from 1895 to 2015.

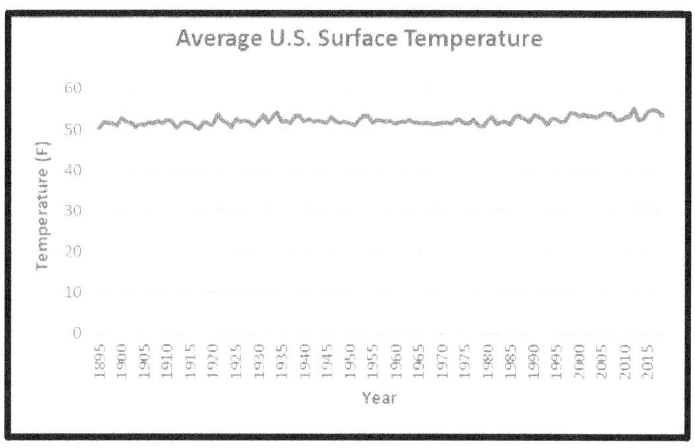

Figure 6. Surface Temperature of the U.S. (zero axis) [142]

We might conclude from this figure that the U.S.'s temperature is not changing all that much. The line seems almost flat, with local variations disguising the relatively small (but significant) change that has occurred. To avoid this misimpression, we might choose a different format that plots the data on a non-zero vertical axis, as in Figure 7.

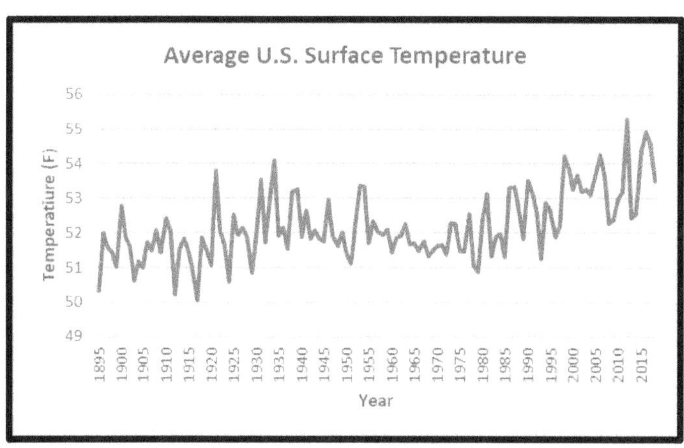

Figure 7. Surface Temperature of the U.S. (non-zero axis)

A designer might choose the first graph if the purpose was to downplay the effects of global warming or the second graph if the intent was to emphasize the effects. A critical reader will always check the axes and the range of numbers they represent.

Lack of Linearity. There is no requirement that an axis on a graph must be like an ordinary ruler with equal spacing between numbers. Sometimes, designers use axes that compress numbers in nonlinear ways. If we don't recognize this possibility, we can sometimes draw very bad conclusions.

For example, Figure 8 shows what the equation y = 10^x looks like when plotted on linear x and y axes.

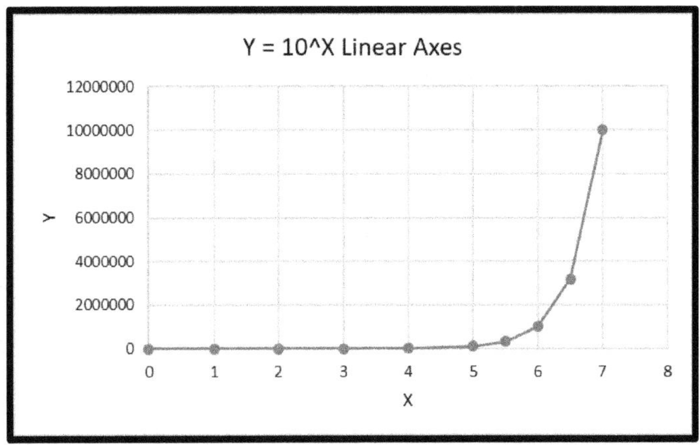

Figure 8. Plot of the Equation Y = 10^X on Linear Axes

Figure 9, on the other hand, shows the same data plotted on a graph with a non-linear y axis.

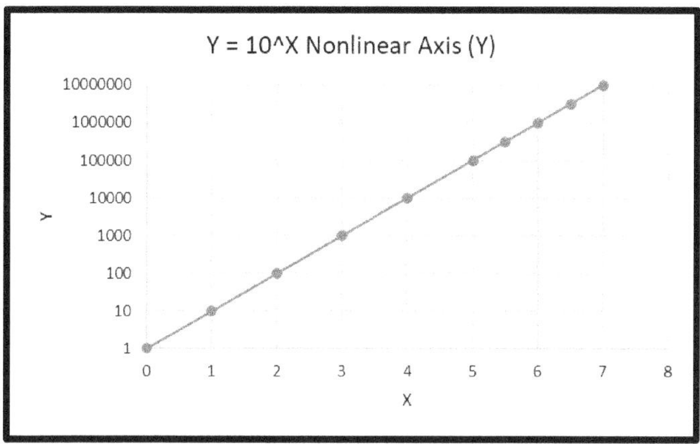

Figure 9. Plot of the Equation Y = 10^X on a Log-Linear Scale.

On the linear x axis of Figure 8, the distance between 0 and 1 is the same as the distance between 1 and 2. On the linear y axis, the distance between 0 and 200,000 is the same as the distance between 200,000 and 400,000. In Figure 9, on the other hand, the x axis is linear, but the y axis is logarithmic (in base 10). On the linear x axis, the distance between 0 and 1 is the same as the distance between 1 and 2, as in the first graph. But on the nonlinear y axis, the distance between 1 and 10 is the same as the distance between 10 and 100. In other words, each step (1, 10, 100, 1000,) is an order of magnitude change. Such displays are easy to misinterpret. The point is to make sure we know how the data is plotted before looking at the shape of the relationship.

Not Showing all of the Data. By selectively choosing (or cherry picking) data, we can make a very sloppy distribution look very well behaved, and convey the impression that there is little variability over time, or that our measurements are tightly correlated to one another.[143] For example, imagine that we took a series of measurements of two related variables and created the following table.

Variable 1	Variable 2
7	2
2	8
4	3
8	4
10	7
6	6
5	5
9	1
3	9
1	10

Table 2. Data Collected for Variables 1 and 2 in a Hypothetical Experiment

We decide to plot them in order to get a better feel for how the two variables are related. Here is our plot (Figure 10):

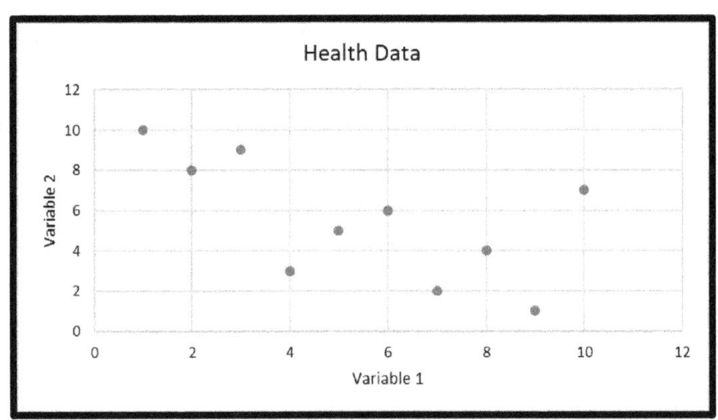

Figure 10. Graph Showing All of the Data Collected

As we look at these points, we begin to wonder about the two points (4,3) and (10,7) that seem out of line. After a bit of thought, we convince ourselves that these two points were probably errors in measurement and should be eliminated. When we redo the numbers, we get this new graph (Figure 11):

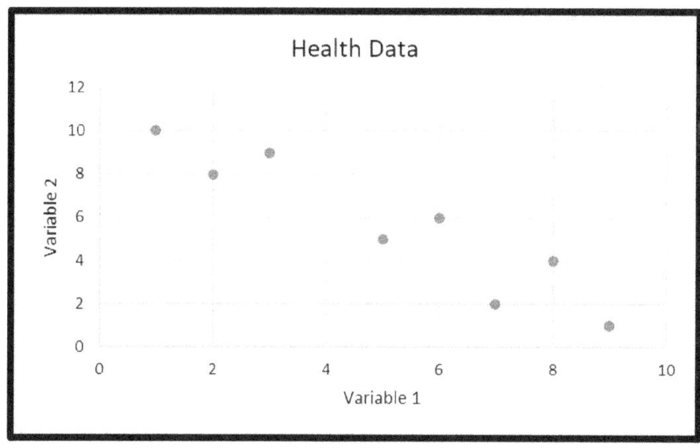

Figure 11. Graph Showing the Data after Cherry Picking

At this point, it is far easier to convince ourselves that there is a strong straight-line relationship between the two variables. But in fact, the numbers come from a random number generator. This is the danger of cherry picking and why good researchers rigidly follow predetermined protocols and do not second guess their data.

Extrapolation. The process of extending the trend, or extrapolation, is often used as a means of predicting what might occur in the future. We might, for example, have a historical plot of a stock index and wonder what it's value might be a year later. An obvious technique would be to extend the line. Imagine, for example, that in January 2018 we saw the following historical graph of the NASDAQ index (Figure 12):

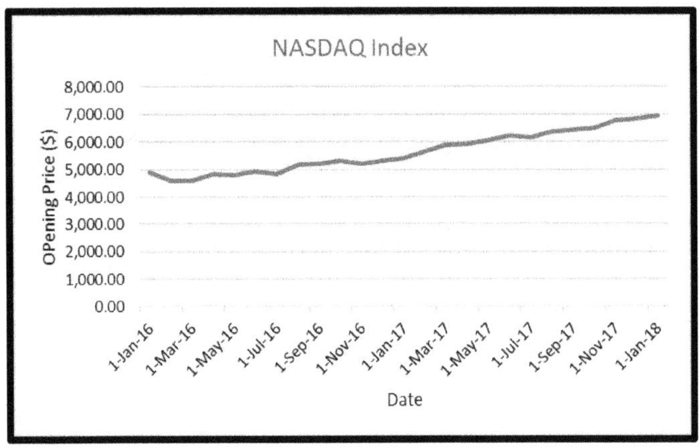

Figure 12. NASDAQ Index from January 2016 to January 2018

Noting this upward trend, we might be tempted to buy a mutual fund that mimics the NASDAQ index. But what would it be worth in a year? We could extend (or extrapolate) the current trend for another year, as the dashed line in Figure 13 shows. This extrapolation suggests that if we bought the fund now, we would reap a tidy profit of about 20% on our investment.

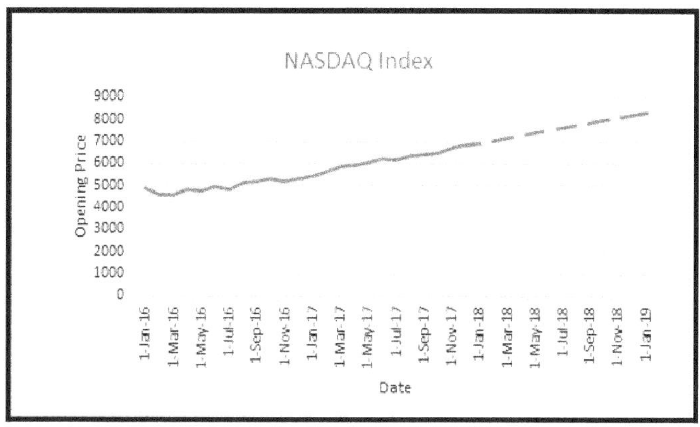

Figure 13. Extrapolation of NASDAQ Index to January 2019

But that is not what happened (Figure 14). The index did not continue upward. Instead, it started to plummet in September:

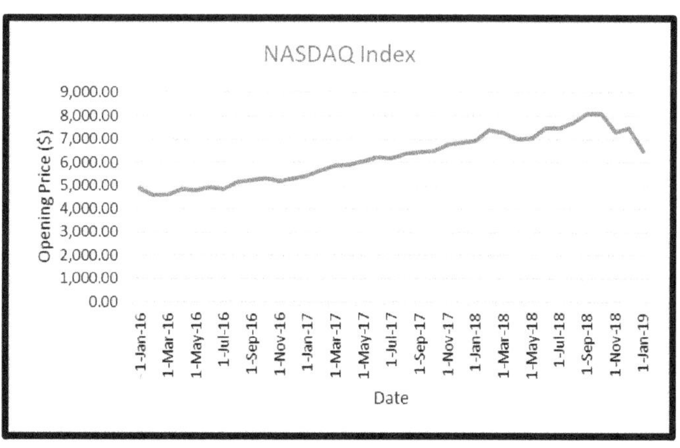

Figure 14. NASDAQ Index from January 2016 to January 2019

In January 2019, we now faced a slight loss instead of our expected gain. And if we extrapolated the trend from the previous three months, it would suggest that the NASDAQ index was going to tank. We could lose a lot of our investment. Do we sell? Here's what happened in the next few months (Figure 15):

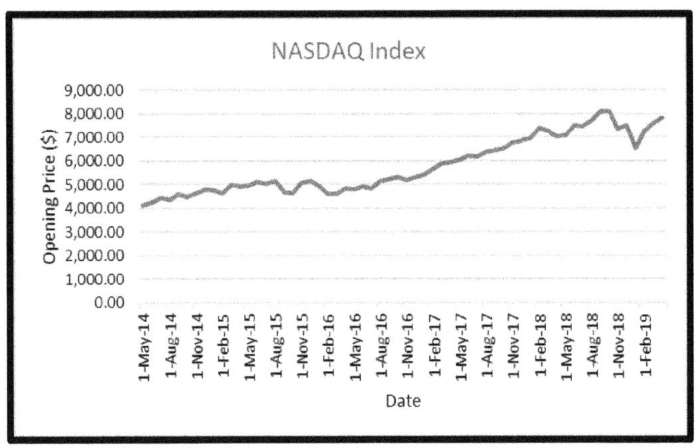

Figure 15. NASDAQ Index from January 2016 to April 2019

At this point, it looks as if things are getting back on track. Selling would have been a bad decision.

Extrapolation can be a dangerous business because no one knows what they don't know. Be wary of any information that depends on extending a graph past its last data point. Extrapolation only makes sense when we have sufficient information about the future and how that might change the current trend.

We are a visual species, and the use of graphs and other visual techniques can be very valuable when words and numbers are inadequate. But graphs bring a whole host of dangers to those who are trying to determine what they know and how they know it. I've covered only a few graphical pitfalls here, simply to emphasize that there are traps in graphs.[144] If you are interested in studying this field, a recent book on the subject is Albert Cairo's *How Charts Lie: Getting Smarter about Visual Information*.[145] Cairo is the Knight Chair of Visual Journalism at the School of Communication at the University of Miami.

Zero and Risk

As a society, we are often a bit obsessed with the number zero, particularly when it comes to our health. We want the concentration of questionable substances in our drinking water to be zero. We want the amount of residual pesticide in our food to be zero. We want the air we breathe to have zero pollutants. We want the risk of a medical intervention to be zero. We want our exposure to chemicals emitted from home construction materials and furniture to be zero. And so on.

But it is all a fiction at some level. The food we eat and the water we drink and the air we breathe can all be tested for contaminants, but finding zero only means that the sample contains less than the minimum amount that the instrument can detect. Similarly, the statistical methods that look for side effects in medical interventions or chemical exposure can only be so sensitive. We can never prove that there is zero chance of a problem. To expect otherwise is to believe in magic.

Those who have a bent against science or technology often fall back on the so-called precautionary principle, or *better safe than sorry*. If one does not know that the negative consequences of a technology are nil, then it should be discarded. For example, the consequences of GMOs are not completely known, so they should be banned.

Such beliefs ignore the fact that practical decisions are not made on the basis of whether or not something is completely safe, but rather on the basis of the benefit it provides relative to the risk it poses. GMOs, for example, will likely have some unintended bad consequences, but they are also an important strategy for feeding the world and dealing with the consequences of climate change.[146]

We live with so much risk each day that our anxiety over lower-probability long-term risks can sometimes seem a bit misplaced.[147] We drive cars daily for their convenience and utility, and yet that activity kills about 40,000 people in the U.S. per year and injures close to 4 million.[148] We encourage our children to play sports, yet that activity produces about 3.5 million injuries in any given year.[149] We drink alcohol with abandon, yet in many ways it is a far more dangerous drug than heroin or crack.[150]

No matter what we do, there will always be risks associated with benefits. And sometimes bad things will happen. In the early years of polio vaccines, for example, one of the vaccine manufacturers unintentionally produced a product containing live vaccine that was given to over 200,000 children. Of those who received the vaccine: 70,000 became sick, 200 were permanently paralyzed to varying degrees, and 10 died.[151] Injury and death from a preventable error like this is tragic. But to provide some perspective, more than 3,000 died from polio infection in the U.S in 1952, three years before vaccinations began.[152]

Some of the most difficult decisions occur when the risk is borne largely by the individual, but the benefit is societal. Such is the case with the current vaccine controversies. Medical problems like measles and flu require herd immunity, but understanding the real and imagined risks of vaccination can be difficult for individuals. Getting an honest, accurate answer to *what do we know and how do we know it?* can help us understand the consequences of a decision to vaccinate or not. But a shift in thinking about risk from "me" to "us" is not always easy.[153]

The Trouble With Percentages

Percent is one of the most misunderstood and misused terms in daily life. We often forget that a percentage is a fraction and don't bother to think much about the numerator and denominator separately. Take the example of bottles of shampoo selling for 33% off the regular price or 50% more for the same price. Which is the better deal? It turns out that they both have the same value.

Let's say that the shampoo is packaged in 8-ounce bottles selling normally at $3.00 and discounted to $2.00 (33% off the regular price) and 12-ounce bottles selling at $3.00 (50% more at the regular price). The better value is the one that is cheapest per ounce:

- For the 8-ounce bottle, the cost per ounce = $$2.00/8 ounces, or $0.25/ounce.
- For the 12-ounce bottle, the cost per ounce = $3.00/12 ounces, or = $0.25/ounce.

This example is perhaps confusing because the two percentages reflect two different bases of comparison; in the first case, cost, and in the second case, weight. As a result, a direct comparison of 33% and 50% is meaningless. Both need to be converted to a cost per ounce in order to make a direct comparison.

Percentages can also mislead when groups of widely varying size are directly compared. For example, we might hear that some particular town has an extremely high incidence of a rare disease. But this does not always mean that there is something wrong with the location. Instead, the anomaly is often the result of a small base population that increases the percentage.

Consider, for example, a disease that normally has a one-in-a-million average occurrence (0.0001%) in the population. Now consider a town of 1,000 inhabitants where — by chance alone— one poor soul has the disease. On a chart comparing the incidence of the disease with location, that town of 1,000 people will appear to be a hotbed, with an incidence 1,000 times as great as the normal percentage. When we see a high incidence statistic, we should always ask if it isn't simply the result of the arithmetic.

And, finally, when someone says our risk of something bad has increased by 100 percent, don't automatically panic. In and of itself, a doubling or tripling of some consequence is often inconsequential in the larger context, because the base risk is very low.[154] We need to ask what a doubling or tripling of risk means in practical terms.

For example, Florida has one of the highest per capita death rates from lightning strikes in the U.S., while the District of Columbia is somewhere in the middle of the pack. The death rate is roughly 4.5 times higher in Florida than D.C., so a legitimate headline might read: *moving to Florida from D.C increases the risk of dying from a lightning strike by 350%.* In fact, this simply means that our move increased our odds of dying from lightning strikes from about 1 in 8 million to 4.5 in 8 million.[155] Florida's population is around 20 million, so about 11 people die from lightning strikes each year. Certainly, no reason to pass up that time at the beach or the golf course. You are probably more likely to die in a car wreck on the trip to and from the destination.

There's a simple way to make sure we are not being misled by percentages. When someone uses a percentage, always ask: (1) percentage of what? and (2) how were the numerator and denominator chosen?

The Trouble With Averages

Averages are an attempt to summarize something that varies, such as the test scores of a group of school children. The most common average is the arithmetic mean, calculated by adding all of the values (all of the test scores) and dividing them by the total number of elements (school children in this example). How could something this simple lead us astray?

One common misimpression is that the arithmetic mean is somehow a typical value. But the degree to which the arithmetic mean is typical of a population depends on the distribution itself.[156] For example, if the average score for a class test was 50, did everyone get a 50 on the test or did half of them get 0 and half of them get 100? It is entirely possible for the arithmetic mean to be a number than no one has in the population. Thus, it is generally safer to think of the arithmetic mean as a measure of central tendency, rather than the typical value.

Another source of confusion lies in the different types of averages that exist. For example, a politician could say that the average income in the U.S. in 2017 was $48,150 or $31,786, and be correct in either case. The difference lies in how the average was calculated.

The first figure represents the arithmetic mean (total U.S. income divided by the population). This average is misleading in some contexts, however, because it is strongly influenced by the small fraction of very high incomes.

An alternative measure of average income is the median, or middle value. Simply line up everyone in the U.S. according to income and pick the middle value. Half the people have an income below this number (the median) and half have an income above it. In 2017 the median income per capita was $31,786, the second figure in our example. Which average our hypothetical politician choses to use likely depends on his or her intent. [157]

Thus, one key to interpreting averages is recognizing that they do not tell the entire story. What's missing is the shape and extent of the distribution that they are characterizing. Statisticians have developed a range of measures for characterizing these other factors, but in my own mind, nothing beats a graph of the data to give me a sense of the distribution. The more skew in a distribution, the more the arithmetic mean and median will differ.

Finally, averages often cause trouble when they are extrapolated from one group to another. A study to determine average caffeine consumption in the U.S. by polling college students, for example, would not necessarily apply to the country as a whole.[158] Yet people often take an average computed from one set of subjects and misapply it to another. A pollster who conducts a phone survey does not sample the entire population, but rather people who: (1) answer their phone when they don't recognize the caller, and (2) are willing to spend time taking telephone surveys.[159]

As in the case of percentages, always ask how the calculation of the average was done. Otherwise, pundits can create a relatively impenetrable cloud of confusion using percentages and averages.

Probability and Intuition

Probability does not come naturally to most people. It is often counterintuitive, causing an extraordinary amount of confusion and more than a few expletives.

One of the best examples of intuition and probability driving people nuts is the Monty Hall problem. This problem is based the 60s/70s tv game show, *Let's Make a Deal,* as hosted by Monty Hall. The format of the show was as follows:

- There are 3 closed doors (1 through 3). Behind one of them is a new car. Behind the other two are goats or some other prize of relatively little value.
- The contestant picks one of the doors (let's say, number 1).
- Monty Hall then opens one of the remaining two doors, revealing a goat.
- The contestant must then decide whether to keep the original choice or choose the other unopened door.

Most people will reason like this: there are two doors left so I have a 50:50 chance. If I change doors, I still have a 50:50 chance. But that common-sense intuitive reasoning is not quite right.

While our intuition tells us that this is a simple choice between two equally likely options, it is actually a more complex problem about changing decisions in light of new evidence. If the contestant chooses the other door, the odds of success improve to 2 out of 3.[160]

Here is another way to think about the problem. Instead of 3 doors, imagine that there are 1,000 doors. We pick one (that conceals either a goat or the car) and Monty eliminates 998 others that definitely do not have the car behind them. Do we still think the odds are even between the two remaining doors — the one we picked and the one that is left? Probability says we should switch since Monty has just given us an overwhelming amount of new information. We now have a choice between a keeping a door we selected when the odds were 1-in-1,000 of picking the winning door, versus the remaining door kept in the running by a host who knows where the car is.[161]

If this still makes no sense, do not be discouraged. When the Monty Hall problem appeared in a popular news column years ago, it created quite a debate. Lots of people (including some who should have known better) got it wrong.

As the examples in the next two sections of this chapter will show, knowing a bit of probability theory can help make good life decisions. Unfortunately, while there are many high school and college textbooks that deal with probability, they can be very tough to understand. A better introductory starting point might be the Khan Academy course on high school probability.[162]

Probability and Gambling Risks

Casino owners are fond of saying that they never take risks. Instead, they make money by getting other people to take risks. Over the long term, it is probability that ensures them a profit. If our long-term financial planning involves success in gambling, then we need to look closely at the math.

Consider a common form of gambling like the lottery. The odds of winning the grand prize in a large lottery such as Powerball ® are on the order of 1 in 300,000,000. Essentially zero. Buy 10 ten tickets and the odds are 1 in 30,000,000, also essentially zero.

But surely if we bought enough tickets every week and were just a wee bit lucky, we would hit the jackpot? Not really. Here is the question that the proponents of lotteries probably don't want us to answer:

> *If someone bought one Powerball ® lottery ticket for each drawing and did this from the time they were 18 until they died at 90, what would the odds be that he or she would win the big prize?*

The answer is 1 in 39,000. Alternatively, it would take about 39,000 lifetimes to win.[163] Clearly, those odds are abysmal. We could, of course, buy more tickets. But in order for us to have even a 1 in 2 chance of winning during our lifetime, we would need to buy more than 19,000 tickets for each drawing.[164] People who routinely ask themselves what they really know and why they know it do not depend on the lottery because they understand how dismal the odds are.[165]

Does that mean we should never play the lottery? Absolutely not. For those who know the math, the lottery is less about probability than hope or possibility. If we want to play, we should do so modestly and enjoy the dreams of the possible that it offers, however improbable. This enjoyment doesn't require spending a lot of money on a lot of tickets on a lot of games. Buy just one ticket for the largest pot that is available.[166] And then enjoy fantasizing about that island in the Caribbean.

Back-Of-The-Envelope Calculations[167]

During a visit to a remote national lab years ago, I commented on the good fortune of the lab workers who rarely faced any significant traffic jams or other commuting problems. One of the lab managers who hosted me then mentioned that an extra minute of commuting each way per day was equivalent to an 8-hour day per year. My immediate reaction was "that can't be right." But then I started thinking: get in a car, drive for one minute, get out, work the day, get back in the car, drive for one minute, and get out of the car. Figuring on 50 weeks per year, times 5 work days per week, times 2 minutes per day, and I arrived at a bit more than 8 hours. At the time, my one-way commute in DC was running 60-90 minutes. Not good.

This estimate is one of the simplest examples of a back-of-the-envelope calculation. Such problems and their solutions are sometimes called *Fermi problems*, in honor of Enrico Fermi, who raised the problem-solving technique to an art form. While Fermi problems usually do not provide an exact solution, they can be far better than simply taking on faith that something will work out. The insight that such estimates can provide and the discipline they enforce in our thinking can often pull us safely back from technical, political, or financial fantasy land.

Fermi was a great teacher, and he took this way of thinking into the classroom. The classic problem that he and other physics teachers used to illustrate these calculations in the 1950s was to determine how many piano tuners lived in Chicago.

At first glance, figuring out how many piano tuners lived in 1950's Chicago might seem like an impossible problem. Without cheating and looking up the number in a 1950's Chicago phonebook, it would seem that the best we could do is to pull a number out of thin air. But many of the problems that we face are like this, so it's worthwhile to learn how to make such problems tractable.

While the piano-tuner problem was used by Fermi and others in the 1950s, its timeless aspect is the way that such a problem can be broken down into a series of questions that we *can* answer. To get a ballpark estimate, we would need to know the following information:

- the approximate population of Chicago in the 1950s,
- roughly how many people were in a family,
- roughly how many families owned pianos,
- roughly how often pianos were tuned,
- roughly how many days a piano tuner worked each year,
- roughly how many pianos a tuner could adjust in a day.

Each of these individual problems can be answered to some degree, either by analogy, reference, or estimation.

Table 3 shows some estimates and calculations that suggest Chicago had about 75 piano tuners in the 1950s. The population of Chicago at that time was around 3 million. Assuming 4 people per family would yield 750,000 families. It might be reasonable to assume that 1-in-10 families owned pianos at that time, creating a need to tune 75,000 pianos. If a piano is tuned on average once every two years, then 37,500 pianos would be tuned each year. If we further assume that piano tuners can tune 2 pianos per day and work 250 days per year, then Chicago needed 75 piano tuners in the 1950s.

VARIABLE	QUANTITY OF INTEREST	ESTIMATE	CALCULATION
A	POPULATION OF CHICAGO IN THE 1950S	3,000,000	
B	NUMBER OF PEOPLE IN A FAMILY	4	
C	NUMBER OF FAMILIES IN CHICAGO (A/B)		750,000
D	FRACTION OF FAMILIES WHO OWNED PIANOS	0.1	
E	NUMBER OF PIANOS (C*D)		75,000
F	AVERAGE TIMES PER YEAR A PIANO IS TUNED	0.5	
G	NUMBER OF PIANOS TO TUNE IN A YEAR (E*F)		37,500
H	NUMBER OF PIANOS A TUNER CAN TUNE IN A DAY	2	
I	NUMBER OF DAYS PER YEAR A TUNER WORKS	250	
J	NUMBER OF PIANOS A TUNER CAN TUNE IN A YEAR (H*I)		500
	NUMBER OF PIANO TUNERS IN CHICAGO (G/J)		75

Table 3. Fermi Approach to the Piano-Tuner Problem

The Chicago yellow pages a number of years ago listed 28 entities under piano tuning and repair. The number "75" is not "28," of course, but the closeness is somewhat amazing considering where we started. One tries to get into the ballpark with a Fermi problem rather than seek an exact figure. Sometimes, just knowing the order of magnitude of a quantity can help us to make better decisions.

Fermi problems are also exceptionally helpful in giving us some sense of where the errors lie and how close our answer might be. If it turns out that we get a better estimate for the population of Chicago, for example, then we can adjust for it. Fermi problems are often less about the final number, and more about where the critical knowledge for a better estimate might lie.

The key to using back-of-the-envelope calculations is recognizing that the process is nothing like a guess. It is a way of calibrating our thinking by reducing uncertainty and getting a feel for a problem. In most significant problems, we do not have all of the data and we don't have forever to accumulate it, yet we would really like to know how close we are and where the uncertainties lie.

An Example from Medical Statistics Most of us have had a medical test at some point that indicated a problem, but on further testing, showed that the initial result was a false alarm. While such experiences can be stressful, they are a consequence of the nature of tests (there are almost always false alarms) and the actual prevalence of the disease being tested. A simple back of the envelope calculation shows how this can happen.

Let's assume that we have reached that magical age of fifty when our doctor starts suggesting that we should have our intestines checked for colorectal cancer. This is the dreaded colonoscopy — a unpleasant 2-day process that involves a lot of diarrhea.

Recently, a new type of colon screening test hit the market that can help some folks avoid the invasive procedure, or at least put it off for a bit. But it might cause a great deal of anxiety in the form of false alarms. Here's why.

According to the manufacturer, the test can err in two directions:[168]

- The false positive rate is 13%. That is, for every 100 people who are tested who do not have colorectal cancer or a precancerous condition, the test will incorrectly report a problem for 13 of them. The test will correctly report no problem for the remaining 87.

- The false negative rate is 8%. That is, for every 100 people who are tested who have colorectal cancer, the test will miss 8 of them. The test will correctly detect the colorectal cancer 92% of the time.[169]

A person takes the test and receives a positive test result. What is the likelihood that he or she really has a problem?

According to American Cancer Society researchers, the incidence of new colon cancer cases for patients 50-54 years old is on the order of 33 per 100,000 people per year.[170] Let's assume that we select 1,000,000 people of this age at random (who have not been diagnosed with colon cancer) and give each of them this test:

- Approximately 330 of these people will have colon cancer and 999,670 will not (this is the 33 per 100,000 incidence number, extended to 1,000,000 people).
- Of the 330 people who have colon cancer:
    1. 26 will test negative (because the false negative rate is 8%: 0.08* 330 = 26)
    2. The remaining 304 will test positive (330-26 = 304, or 0.92*330 = 304
- Of the 999,670 who do not have colon cancer:
    1. 129,957 will test positive (because the false positive rate is 13%: 0.13*999,670 = 129,957)
    2. The remaining 870,713 will test negative (999,670 – 129,957 = 869,713, or 0.87 * 999,670 = 869,713)

If a person is one of the 130,261 people (129,957 + 304) with a positive test result, then he or she is either one of the 304 who have colon cancer or the 129,957 who do not. The probability that this person who tested positive has colon cancer is the ratio of those who have colon cancer and tested positive to all of those who tested positive:

$$\text{Probability} = 304/130{,}261$$
$$\cong 0.00233$$

So, the odds are about 1 in 429.

This is, of course, only an estimate based on the *big* assumption that we are typical of the population in general (where the 33/100,000 incidence rate applies). Like all Fermi problems, we can redo them with more accurate estimates. For example, we might want to raise the incidence number if we have family history of the disease. Or lower or raise it depending on our race, our habits, and our diet.[171]
At this point, you might recognize that this dominating false alarm effect is similar to the argument that was made earlier about bias in scientific publication and its negative effect when there are lots of possible relationships to test, few true relationships, and a relatively high false positive rate. Both give lots of false alarms. So, in the words that grace the beginning of Douglas Adams' classic, *The Hitchhikers Guide to the Galaxy*: "Don't Panic."[172]

I have not found many good references for back of the envelope calculations. Most that exist, such as Clifford Swartz's *Back of the Envelope Physics*, are not the easiest of reads Perhaps the best place to start would be Lawrence

Weinstein and John Adam's *Guesstimation: Solving the World's Problems on the Back of a Cocktail Napkin.*[173]

We Use More Math Than We Think We Do

When we say things like: "I am no good at math," or I can't do numbers," we are effectively sabotaging ourselves. When we start with negatives like these, we immediately create a hole that we have to dig ourselves out of before we can progress.

The fact is that most of us use math far more than we think we do. Take the dreaded logarithm as an example. Although logarithms probably seem to be one of those "I'll never use this stuff!" topics, we all probably know more about logarithms than we think we do. For example, when we hear a sound intensity described as 90 decibels or 90 dB, or acidity describe as pH of 6, or an earthquake described as a 7 or 8, we are using logarithms. And along with that usage comes some feel for what the numbers mean. Most of us know, for example, that a 1 or 2 magnitude earthquake is no big deal, but that an 8 or 9 will likely be devasting in populated areas.

Perhaps it helps to think of mathematics not as a subject in and of itself, but rather as part of the thinking and decision-making process. As the theoretical mathematician William Thurston said, "mathematics is not about numbers, equations, computations or algorithms; it's about understanding."[174]

CHAPTER SIX

Some Thoughts for the Future

It is a dog-eat-dog world, Sammy, and I'm wearing Milk-Bone underwear — Norm Peterson [175]

In St. Petersburg, Russia, stands a statue to the French architect who designed several of the city's 19th century buildings. Unfortunately, there is a slight problem with this tribute. The statue is really a likeness of an obscure 19th century Scottish chemist rather than the intended architect. The error occurred because the chemist's picture was accidently used in a *Wikipedia* article on the French architect. The sculptor was quoted as saying:

We were confident that the internet would give us the correct information...[176]

One can't help but feel a bit sorry for the sculptor, yet wonder at the same time whether this isn't a glimpse into the future.

The garbage-to-truth ratio of today's sources of information seems to be growing and our attention span is shrinking. Whether the mistakes are innocent (as was likely with the *Wikipedia* entry) or malicious (Vladimir Putin manipulating U.S. elections) doesn't matter. We all run the risk of acting on bad information. And we will pay the consequences, whether it's a lighter wallet, a less-healthy body, a more poorly-run country, or a simply a reputation for being a bit of a blockhead.

Much of this punishment can be avoided by doing a better job of understanding what we know and how we know it. If the previous chapters have done their job, we should now have some inkling of the tricks that our mind and the actions of others can play on us. Here are some final thoughts on how to minimize the damage caused by bad information and poor thinking.

Listen More, Talk Less, Ask Good Questions

Bernard Baruch was an influential 20th century financier and economic advisor to several U.S. Presidents. He once said that most of the successful people he'd known were the ones who did more listening than talking.[177]

Listening and asking good questions in order to better understand someone's point of view can be hard work. It is particularly challenging when we don't necessarily agree with what is being said. But if our conversation ends with the other person saying *I don't care, that is what I believe*, then we have lost. Pointing out logical and factual flaws isn't a way to score points; it is a way to tick somebody off.

How we respond in a conversation can make a huge the difference in the outcome. Instead of challenging everything someone says in some misguided attempt to change their mind, ask non-threatening and respectful questions to better understand their position and perhaps lead them in a more productive direction. Bad is: *You don't know what you are talking about*. Better is: *I wonder what would happen if...* Practice elicitation.

Surround Ourselves With Better Sources of Information

An earlier chapter emphasized the importance of creating a virtual division — surrounding ourselves with reliable people and other information sources that help us to understand issues and make good decisions. How we think and how we act and what we can accomplish all depend on the tools and methods and knowledge that we have to reason with.[178]

Critical thinking is about solving problems – whether it is trying to live a healthier life, deciding whom to vote for, or making a new investment. We attack such issues with what we know and are familiar with, and it is one reason why it often pays to consult people with different viewpoints and skills. A heart specialist sees a medical condition differently than the patient. A real estate broker views a house in a different light than the person who has lived in it for 20 years. A security specialist will consider threats to our business that we might not even know exist.

Even when we think we know all about an issue, we probably only understand it from the perspectives that we have grown accustomed to. Working with others can broaden that perspective, making it easier to ask what we know and how we know it.

Here is a brain teaser that nicely illustrates how easily we can sometimes miss the point.

> *A man enters a bar and asks for a glass of water.*
> *The bartender draws a gun and shoots into the ceiling.*
> *The man thanks him and walks out.*

What just happened? The puzzle is known the glass-of-water paradox, and unless we happen onto the right perspective, it can tie us in knots. The answer is that the man had the hiccups.[179]

One of the best feelings in the world is when someone gives us an entirely new perspective on an old problem and we react with: *I never thought about it that way!*

Aggressively Explore New Ideas

While I was managing programs for the government, my most successful projects usually started out with a handful of possibilities, but no clear path forward. My teams would attack all of the options, trying to understand the weaknesses and strengths in each approach. Most of the attacks were failures, but eventually we'd learn from those mistakes and move forward.

Considering ideas that don't work out is a good and necessary part of critical thinking, as long as we learn from the failures and don't try to hang on to the ideas too long. Knowing when to stop believing or working on something is essential, and the more time and effort and ego we have in something, the harder it is to let go.[180]

When we are not afraid to experiment and fail, we consider lots of different things. Peter Sims, for example, wrote an entire book on the idea of making little bets, or trying new ideas in small ways. One of his examples was the HP-35, the world's first scientific pocket calculator.[181] The Hewlett-Packard Company developed the calculator, but then had to decide what to do with the research. The calculator would be very expensive, and HP's marketing experts told co-founder Bill Hewlett that it wouldn't sell. Rather than accept the large risk or scrap the project, Hewlett asked: "Why don't we build a thousand and see what happens?" They did, and shortly after HP was selling a thousand HP-35s *every day*.[182]

Lose the Ego

When Nobel-Prize winner Daniel Kahneman was asked to describe the most damaging flaw that plagues good decision making, he answered: *overconfidence*. While he was not optimistic that we could ever completely contain it, he saw this deficiency as the source of misguided optimism that often leads to poor decisions.[183]

Overconfidence is unsupported belief that we are right about something. When we are overconfident, we don't bother to take the time to ask: "but, what about," or, "what if? As a result:

- We are sure we can competently text and drive at the same time.
- We can quit smoking or drinking or vaping or doping any time we want.
- We don't need insurance because nothing bad is going to happen to us.
- We can drive safely in the worst weather and traffic conditions because we are such good drivers.
- We don't need computer backup because our computer never crashes.
- We believe that everyone should have *our* values and ethics.
- If someone breaks into our house and threatens us, we'll just shoot them with our handgun that rarely or never sees a gun range.
- We don't need to study for the test because we already know the material.
- We can eat whatever we want because chronic diseases are something other people get.
- We always know what is best for us and others.

Living in Colorado, I see an abundance of overconfidence in tourists, especially at our National Parks. Every year, the news is the same. The body of hiker is found on an isolated mountain peak. A skier is killed by an avalanche in a backcountry no-ski zone. A swimmer drowns in a mountain lake. The Park Service cautions visitors by posting warnings that include the stark reality that *the mountains don't care.* The critical thinkers who read these posted warnings immediately hike back to their cars for rain jackets, water, communications gear, and other supplies. The overconfident just take off down the trail.[184]

Of course, none of this means that confidence is necessarily bad. Informed confidence creates new businesses, explores new environments, and sets new records. But striking the right balance between confident and overconfident is an exercise in asking ourselves what we know and how we know it. This is often difficult, and requires that we are as honest as we can be with ourselves. If we all left a little room for doubt in our conclusions, we would do a far better job of determining what we really know and how we know it.

Be Self Critical

We generally find it easier to find fault with the thinking of others than with our own. But if we want to make more effective personal decisions, we need a healthy dose of introspection and self-criticism.

Leonardo da Vinci was arguably one of the more thoughtful people who ever lived. While he is known for many things, perhaps his paintings (such as the *Mona Lisa* that sits in the Louvre) are his best-known works. He was also a prolific writer who documented his thoughts and insights throughout his life in notebooks. In the 6,000 or so notebook pages that survive, one of them provides the following advice on self-criticism to fellow painters.[185]

> *We know well that mistakes are more easily detected in the works of others than in one's own...I say that when you are painting you should take a flat mirror and often look at your work with it, and it will then be seen in reverse, and will appear to be by the hand of some other master, and you will be better able to judge its faults than in any other way.*
>
> *It is also a good plan every now and then to go away and have a little relaxation; for then when you come back to the work your judgement will be surer since to remain constantly at work will cause you to lose the power of judgement.*
>
> *It is also advisable to go some distance away, because the work always appears smaller, and more of it is taken in at a glance, and a lack of harmony or proportion in the various parts and in the colours of the object is more readily seen.*

If we substitute our own thinking on an issue for the painting that da Vinci is focused on, we have some pretty good advice for making better decisions. A different perspective on an issue (perhaps looking at the issue from someone else's viewpoint), letting some time pass before making a final judgement (things often look very different after a good night's sleep, for example), and creating distance (stand back and see the issue as part of a bigger picture) are good general guidance for any critical thought.

Will Any of This Matter When the Machines Take Over?

Predicting the future is a dangerous game, but it seems fair at this point to speculate a bit on how the nature of decision making might change in the future. Advances in computing and artificial intelligence (AI) are clearly following very rapid growth curves. As a result, we will make more and more of our future decisions with computer assistance that is designed to present, calculate, suggest, alert, and even nudge us in certain directions. Sound nutty? We should all take a hard look at our evolving relationships with Alexa or Google Assistant.

There is no doubt that these changes will be highly disruptive to our lifestyles and employment. But it might help to understand that this type of change has been creeping up on us for a very long time.

Consider, for example, how driving a car has evolved over the past 70-80 years. In the 1940s and 1950s, for example, drivers had to worry about things like: when to shift, how to set a throttle, how to maintain a steady speed, not getting too close to the person in front, and not falling asleep at the wheel. If you had a really old car like a 1930's Model A Ford, you even had to manually adjust the spark advance on the ignition. Do it wrong, and you could snap the bolts off of the starter![186]

Today, such tasks and much more are done for us, or at least we are helped in our efforts to do them. The vast majority of modern cars, for example, have automatic transmissions and cruise control. If we nod off, deviate from our lane, or have other vehicles in our blind spots, our cars let us know. Our cars can brake for us, parallel park, and even sense a crash and protect us from impact injury. Thus, how we drive today is far more a shared responsibility between ourselves and the intelligence that is embedded in the car.

The car is in some ways a model for the future of how most collaborative critical thinking will go, including answering those essential *what do we know and how do we know it*? questions. Just like driving, thinking and making decisions is becoming a more shared responsibility between ourselves and the intelligence that is embedded in the tools we use. Whether we are doctors, lawyers, engineers, tax accountants, scientists, mechanics, carpenters, writers, teachers, or salesmen, AI-driven machines will be in our decision loops, providing information, doing *what if?* analyses, identifying our biases, vetting information, looking for deception, and correcting our logic. More and more of the decisions that we make – whether work related, personal, financial, medical, or recreational — will be joint decisions.[187]

We'll still be asking what we know and how we know it, but with (effectively) a far more robust and extensive virtual division backing us up.

Not everyone sees these future changes as overwhelmingly beneficial. Some, like Tesla and SpaceX CEO Elon Musk, see A.I. machines as "far more dangerous than nukes." because they could become too strong for humans to control.[188]. The well-known physicist Stephen Hawking expressed similar beliefs before his death in 2018.

On the other hand, others take a less apocalyptic view of intelligent machine capabilities. Pomona College Professor of Economics Gary Smith, who authored *The A.I. Delusion*, thinks that fears of a machine-dominated world are unfounded.[189] He suggests that the biggest danger might lie in unjustified confidence in machines:

> *We fear that super-intelligent machines will decide to protect themselves by enslaving or eliminating humans. But the real danger is not that computers are smarter than us, but that we think computers are smarter than us and, so, trust computers to make important decisions for us.*

From my perspective, it is far too early to tell which vision of the future will ultimately prevail. But I suspect that Professor Smith's vision will be closer to the mark, at least for the foreseeable future.

Even more reason to keep asking what we know and how we know it.

Summing Up

In his book, *The Changing Culture of a Factory*, Canadian social scientist Eliott Jaques noted:

> *...each one of us, in the course of development, has painfully worked out a set of assumptions as to what is real and what is important in determining our behavior; secondly, that these assumptions give*

meaning to our lives and offer some protection from fear and uncertainty; and, thirdly, that even personal attempts to modify such deeply-rooted assumptions arouse anxiety and resistance which can only be overcome by serious psychological effort.[190]

Jaques understood that it is hard to deal with life's baggage and not so easy to change. But it would be tragic if we didn't try to continue to grow and learn and adapt. The good news is that we have something to say about the person we are yet to become.

I started this book asking the following questions about making better decisions:

- What forces are at work when we think or reason about an issue?
- How are we manipulated to believe and act in certain ways?
- How should we evaluate different sources of information?
- Why is science so controversial?
- How do numerical concepts help and harm reasoning?

I am hopeful that my attempt to expand on these questions has inspired some of us to read, listen, and reason a bit more critically and humbly. We all need to be more aware of how we weigh and consider information. Who knows what we — young and old — could accomplish as a society if enough of us actually did so.

Appendices

Cognitive Biases

Logical Fallacies

Elicitation Techniques

Appendix A

Cognitive Biases

Cognitive biases are mental processes that lead us astray and keep us from making better decisions. Unlike logical fallacies, these biases are not necessarily a mistake in reasoning, but rather influences in one direction or another. They distort our objectivity.

On the order of a hundred different types of cognitive biases exist. Here are some that can significantly degrade our ability to accurately know what we know and how we know it. Each starts with an example, followed by an explanation.

We always eat at the same restaurant! Ambiguity effect is the preference for options with known consequences. For example, we eat at the same places or take the same way to work every day instead of exploring new options. In a sense, this is a tendency to equate unknown information with negative information.

This dress is normally priced at $500. Anchoring bias occurs when the first piece of data we get becomes our calibration point. In the above example, $200 sale price probably looks pretty once we have anchored on $500.

Hello, Alexa. Anthropomorphism is the tendency to ascribe human traits to animals, objects, and concepts. One has to wonder where this bias will lead us in the future as more and more computer devices take on human traits.

I won't swim at the beach because I might get bitten by a shark. Availability heuristic is the tendency to make judgements about the likelihood or magnitude of events based on how easily examples come to mind. This can distort our ability to judge, for example, the frequency of some occurrence (The odds of someone being killed by a shark in their lifetime are about 1 in 3.7 million, but any attack makes the news.).[191]. We see this bias strongly in the degree to which the media has created misimpressions about crime, poverty, education and natural disasters.

A simple lie told once may not be well received. But tell the lie a thousand times and it will be believed.[192] Availability cascade is the idea that if something is said often enough in public discussion, it will become true in the public mind. Almost all campaigns for public office use this technique to some extent.

Everyone I know believes that this guy is a crook, so I think he is too. Bandwagon effect is the bias toward believing something because many other people do. The bandwagon effect can lead to group think, in which a group makes bad decisions out of a desire for conformity, the avoidance of controversy, or laziness.

You are sometimes very sociable and other times, an introvert. The Barnum effect occurs when someone perceives a general description as being very accurate for them personally. This is, in part, how astrologists and fortune tellers make their living.

That is a compelling argument. It definitely leads to the right conclusion. Belief bias occurs when we believe an argument is sound because the conclusion sounds right. Political arguments are often accepted this way.

We are the only unbiased people in this room. Bias blind spot is our ability to more easily spot bias in others than in ourselves.

Have you noticed how often 24, 26, and 28 show up in the Powerball lottery? Clustering illusion is when we tend to see patterns when none are there. For example, seeing a trend in randomly picked lottery numbers.

This is just one more sign that we are up against a conspiracy. Confirmation bias is the tendency to interpret new information in ways that confirm our prior beliefs.

Obama is a Muslim. Continued-influence effect is the tendency to continue to believe information that has been shown to be incorrect. For example, false information about a politician might continue to influence voters long after it has been debunked.

This country is going to the dogs. Declinism is a tendency to believe that an organization or society is declining and facing a bleak future.

Would you like the large size for only $.50 more? This is a popular marketing play known as the decoy effect. It's why the medium popcorn (a decoy) is sometimes much more expensive than the small size and only slightly less expensive than the large size. The decoy makes the most expensive large size look like a deal.[193]

I made a few dollars on this stock when I sold it. I'll sell the other one once it goes back up to what I bought it for. Disposition effect is the idea that investors will tend to hold assets that are losing value and sell assets that are increasing in value.

I am a very good driver. The problem is everyone else. Dunning–Kruger effect occurs when those with very little knowledge of a subject tend to overestimate their understanding and capability, while those with a great deal of knowledge tend to underestimate their knowledge and capability. Those who need help the most are the least likely to figure that out.

I can't stop now. I've got too much in this. Endowment effect occurs when we tend to overvalue our possessions. Essentially, we want to sell our house for more money than we'd be willing to spend to buy it in the first place. A related effect known as sunk cost occurs when we are less likely to abandon a bad idea when we have invested time and effort in it.

I'm sure he did it. False memory occurs when we recall an imagined incident as real. An entire incident could be imagined or pieces of it could be false. Erroneous eyewitness testimony is one example with especially serious consequences.

I am not voting for her because she is for higher taxes. Focusing effect is when we place too much emphasis on one piece of the bigger picture. For example, we might focus too heavily on one issue of a political candidate's campaign rather than consider the impact of the platform as a whole. Or, we might focus too heavily on past performance of a stock rather than future prospects.

Everyone knows this is true! False consensus is the tendency for us to overestimate how widely our beliefs are held by others. A related bias, *false uniqueness bias,* is the tendency for us to overestimate how unique we are. This can become a problem, for example, when we start to question our "averageness" as an excuse to avoid taking a doctor's advice.

It's their own fault! Fundamental attribution error is the tendency for us to judge others more harshly than ourselves. When something bad happens to someone else, we tend to blame their behavior and discount the circumstances. On the other hand, if the same thing happened to us, we'd tend to downplay our own behavior and blame the event more on circumstances. Remember the old admonition that you cannot understand someone before you walk a walk a mile in their shoes.

We can't allow this demonstration; it's a matter of public safety. Or: we have to allow this

demonstration: it's a matter of free speech. Framing effect occurs when we decide an issue differently, depending on how information is presented to us.

He has a nice smile, so I think he will make a good senator. Halo effect is the tendency to perceive that positive or negative traits carry over from one area to another.

I'll have the fries with that. Hyperbolic discounting occurs when we prefer a smaller reward now over a larger reward in the future. This is why we almost always eat french fries instead of the salad and later complain about our weight and health.

Everyone but us is clueless. In-group bias is the tendency to view people within our group more favorably that those outside of our group, and to give preferential treatment to those within our group. A group can be, for example, political, ethnic, or religious.

Here are two opinion polls that completely contradict each other! Insensitivity to sample size is our tendency to ignore sample size when evaluating a study's conclusion. Other things being equal, a public poll of 100 people is far less reliable than one taken of 10,000 people.

How fast were the cars going when they smashed into one another? Misinformation effects occur when our memory is distorted by information that we learn after an event has occurred. In a police investigation, for example, how questions are worded can distort our memory of a crime. In the above example, the term "smashed into" will elicit a higher speed estimate than terms like "bumped."[194]

No one seems to get this but me. Naïve realism is the mistaken belief that our worldview is reality and anyone who disagrees is misinformed or malicious.[195]

We don't need insurance. This place hasn't flooded for 100 years! Normalcy bias is our tendency to underestimate the probability of a future disaster just because it hasn't happened yet. Things will just continue as they have been, rather than change for the worse.

Our ideas are always the best because we are the only ones who really understand the problem. Not-invented-here bias is our reluctance to accept ideas and products that were developed by outsiders. This is often a criticism of organizations, but it applies equally well to individuals.

This is the third time I've heard that term used today! Observational selection bias is our tendency to notice something more often after something causes us to be aware of it. For example, we read a word that we are unfamiliar with and then notice it again and again shortly thereafter. The word has not suddenly become more prevalent. Instead, we are now primed to notice it. This effect is also called the frequency illusion.

If they don't notice the issue, it's their problem. Omission bias occurs when we consider a harmful act to be worse than not acting, even though the consequences are the same. For example, lying about the condition of the car we are trying to sell is considered worse behavior than not mentioning the mechanical problems.

If we can just pull this off, we'll live like kings! Optimism bias is wishful thinking, or a tendency to overestimate the positive and underestimate the negative. Optimism is not necessarily bad, but it does need to be grounded in reality.

You can't go wrong with this stock. Overconfidence effect is when we are unjustifiably confident of our own actions or answers to questions. Experts such as stock fund managers are particularly susceptible to this effect. Very few of them beat the market over the long term.

This renovation will only take a week. Planning fallacy is our tendency to underestimate how long a task will take. Every nail goes in straight, every board is cut to the right length, and everyone shows up for work on time.

Between the two of us, we can cover the mortgage on this more expensive house. Projection bias occurs when we overestimate how much our future condition will match our current condition. We get the larger mortgage, but run into trouble when one contributor loses his or her job.

What do they know? They are just after profits. Reactive devaluation occurs when we discount information or guidance because it came from someone we dislike or otherwise have problems with. For example, we might refuse to take a medical doctor or pharmaceutical company's advice simply because they are part of the establishment.

All of the data supports this. Selective perception is the idea that we tend to see what we expect or want to see and ignore the rest. For example, we might only remember the parts of the news report that supported our preconceptions.

You academics are all alike. Stereotyping occurs when we assume that a member of a group has certain characteristics without knowing that individual. If we assume, for example, that all university professors live in ivory towers, we eliminate many great sources of practical information.

The primary sources for this appendix are Wikipedia's "List of Cognitive Biases," and Stephen Novella's *The Skeptics' Guide to the Universe: How to Know What's Really Real in a World Increasingly Full of Fake.*[196]

Appendix B

Logical Fallacies

We make logical errors in many different ways. This particular list was compiled using several textbooks and web resources.[197] As in the previous appendix, each one starts with an example, followed by an explanation.

He said that this computer has a terabyte of solid-state internal storage, 10 gigabytes of RAM, and a multicore CPU running at 3.6 gigahertz, so he must know what he is doing. This is *alphabet soup* — the overuse of acronyms and jargon as a strategy for making someone (including ourselves) believe we know what we are talking about. Alphabet soup is common among computer techs, auto mechanics, and salesmen, and especially among government officials. I was once phoned by an Army civilian who talked nonstop in acronyms for 10 minutes. I didn't understand a single noun he used. When I finally got my chance to interrupt him, I was able to confirm that he had the wrong Greg Moore. Perhaps the other Greg Moore was more impressed by the alphabet soup.

He would make a good president because he was successful in business. This is a *non sequitur*, a fallacy in which the conclusion does not follow from the premise. The conclusion assumes that both business and government require the same skills, ignoring key differences between the types of organizations and their goals.

Linus Pauling was a great chemist, so his statements about the medical effects of megadoses of vitamin C must be true. This is *argument from authority* in which the argument must be true because an expert or authority said so, rather than any evidence or reasoning that supports it.

My child would never use drugs! This is *argument from final outcome* or *argument from final consequences.* The fallacy is the idea that something must be true or false not based on its evidence, but rather on whether its consequences are acceptable or not. The argument that our child did something bad is dismissed in this case because it contradicts our strongly-held belief that our child is always good.

You've got to buy some Yahoo stock. Everyone else is. This is *appeal to popularity* that argues we should do something because everyone else is doing it. It is strongly related to the cognitive bias known as the bandwagon effect, or the propensity to believe things because others do.

Smoking causes cancer because the smoke from cigarettes contains carcinogens. This is *circular reasoning.* If the words at the beginning of the statement have essentially the same meaning as those at the end, the argument is circular. It assumes the premise is true.

I took the medicine and my aching shoulder got better in a few weeks. So, the medicine worked. This is *post hoc, ergo propter hoc.* Because something follows something else, it must have been caused by the earlier event. Our aching shoulder could also have gotten better on its own, a common effect known as regression to the mean.

Sales of ice cream and incidence of forest fires are strongly correlated, which proves that ice cream causes forest fires. This is *correlation versus causation*, when two effects can be related without one causing the other. Sale of ice cream and the occurrence of forest fires are strongly correlated, not because one causes the other, but because warm weather is a factor that affects both.

The politician's position on illicit drug use is too strict, since he used drugs as a teenager. This is an example of *tu quoque*, or *you too*, where we consider a claim to be false simply because the person who says it has acted in a manner counter to his assertion in the past.

Look at that face! Would anyone vote for that? or He is temperamentally unfit! These are *ad hominem* remarks, the use of an insult as part of an argument. Both examples are from the 2016 presidential campaign. The first is Republican presidential primary candidate Donald Trump criticizing Republican presidential primary candidate Carly Fiorina's appearance rather than debating her competency. The second is Democratic presidential candidate Hilary Clinton directing attention to Republican presidential candidate Donald Trump's disposition rather than his policies.

It's just common sense! This is an *appeal to common sense*; that is, when we consider something true because it is common sense. As we saw earlier, common sense is sometimes wrong, especially when we are treading on new ground.

There is no evidence of intelligent alien life, so ET does not exist. This is the *ad ignorantiam* fallacy, or argument from ignorance. It assumes that something must be true because there is no evidence to the contrary. The classic example of this fallacy is the old argument that all swans are white because every swan we've seen up to now is white. That all changed with the first discovery of a black swan.

GMOs are extremely harmful. or GMOs are perfectly safe. This is an example of a *false dichotomy*, in which we consider only one extreme or the other in an argument. In the GMO example, the truth probably lies somewhere between these two extremes.

We've always done it this way! This is the *is-ought fallacy* that confuses *what is* with *what ought to be* in an argument. Just because something is a certain way, doesn't mean it should stay that way.

I'm a strong believer in freedom of speech, but Fox News has to go. This is an *inconsistency fallacy* in which two statements are contradictory. Yogi Berra, a well-known baseball catcher, coach, and manager was famous for his inconsistency statements such as: "No one goes there anymore because it is too crowded."

I only buy clothing made from natural fibers. This is an *appeal to nature fallacy* or the idea that natural is always better, rather than arguing on the basis of relevant criteria. Many things in nature can be bad for us and many natural products are inferior to synthetics.

Why not let kids buy tobacco products? They get them anyway. The *nirvana fallacy* occurs when we dismiss a realistic practical option because it isn't a perfect idealized solution. The example draws attention away from the obvious; that is, what might be done to make the laws more effective?

It may be true that the minimum wage should be adjusted, but the real solution is to eliminate burdensome government regulations so businesses can grow and be able to pay their employees higher salaries.[198] This is an example of a *red herring*, or an irrelevant argument that distracts us from the issue. In this case, the question (should the minimum wage be adjusted) is replaced with a rant on government regulation. As the example suggests, it is a very popular tool for the politician who is working hard to not answer a question. How many times have we heard a politician talk for 5 minutes and never answer the question that was asked?

If all of the kids decided to jump off a bridge, would you do it, too? This is a *reductio ad absurdum* fallacy. We often use this example as the classic parental response to "but, all of the other kids did it too!" This fallacy occurs when we try to disprove or counter something by taking its provisions to an absurd level.

More restrictions on gun ownership will eventually lead the government to take away all firearms. This is an example of the *slippery-slope fallacy*, in which we argue that a small change in a particular direction inevitably leads to larger undesirable changes.

If we don't raise the educational budget, we are abandoning our children! This is an example of the *strawman fallacy* in which we argue against a weak or nonexistent position that we have created (abandoning our children), instead of the actual issue (do we need to increase the school budget?).

Obama isn't a citizen; show me his birth certificate. Followed by: this short-form birth certificate is not good enough, where is the long form? Followed by: this long-form certificate is not good enough...This is an example of the *moving goalpost fallacy* that occurs when something is proven or disproven by agreed-upon evidence, and the standard is then changed to avoid conceding the issue.

Appendix C

Elicitation Techniques

A few days before I wrote this section, I was stuck in an airport because of a late plane. A heavy-set man with a briefcase (probably retired or semi-retired) sat down across from me at the gate. He looked slightly familiar, but not enough for me to probe further. Eventually, someone who appeared to be a stranger filled the seat next to him. In a matter of minutes, the older gentleman began talking.

I perked up when I heard the phrase: *I used to work for the government* which is often Washington DC code for *I worked for one of those 3 letter organizations that no one talks about like CIA or FBI or NSA*. Over a period of a half an hour, the older gentleman proceeded to open up, and begin talking about his career. He started with vague references, but eventually got very specific. This outpour took little prompting from the other fellow. Just a bit of feedback now and then some interesting tidbits to show he was a good listener. While I do not know if the younger person's actions were intentional or just natural conversation, they were quite effective at eliciting information.

The government person should have known better. His behavior was all the more ironic because he had apparently worked for the FBI, an organization that has done a particularly good job of making the public aware of elicitation techniques. Their brochure, *Elicitation*, is well worth the time. [199]

Elicitation is the discreet acquisition of information through what appears to be innocuous conversation. Here are some examples and general explanations of the tools that elicitors use.

Yes, that sounds right. Active listening is a good technique for keeping us talking. It includes not only positive verbal feedback that shows that the listener is engaged, but also body language.

Ronald down in processing is on my back to fix his computer, but he isn't in. Can you help me? This is an example of pretending to be an insider. It is a technique that is often used by hackers to get closely-held information such as a password. When targeting an individual in a company, for example, a hacker might know the business jargon and have some information about employees, usually obtained through an earlier elicitation effort. They use this information to gain the target's confidence, and that, in turn, helps them to acquire the information or access they need.[200]

Did you see the prototype? I've heard it is pretty amazing. This is an example of a leading question. While the answer is yes or no, it opens the door to the new product and any information the individual might know.

My kids are like that too. This is an example of how someone might build rapport with us before going after information. The better the rapport, the more comfortable we are talking with them.

That's hard to believe! This is one of the easiest and quickest ways to start the flow of information. It puts us in a position of defending what we just said. Rather than look like a liar, we will tell why our statement was true, revealing details that the elicitor is after.

Keep this to yourself, but... or I really shouldn't tell you this, but...This is *quid pro quo* in which an elicitor shares a bit of somewhat sensitive information in hope that we will reciprocate. The desire to reciprocate or return a favor is very strong. That is (in part) why some charities send us address labels during the holiday season.

I'm not sure I understand. How does that work? In this approach, an elicitor encourages us to expand on what we just said. In the explanation, we are likely to reveal valuable details or insights.

Everybody knows the world is really flat. This is an extreme example of saying something deliberately wrong in order to prompt a correction. This technique works especially well on university professors who might have useful information about a new technology they are trying to patent.

That new product you developed is pure genius. Flattery will get you everywhere. After hearing this, many of us can't wait to toot our own horn.

That must be a tough place to work. This can be an attempt to get us to complain and reveal problems that might exist in a competitive organization.

Of course, not all elicitation is about spying and business competition. Good elicitation can help sales and marketing target products to consumers and even help engineers and designers who are trying to understand the requirements for a new product. It helps us to answer what we know and how we know it.

About the Author

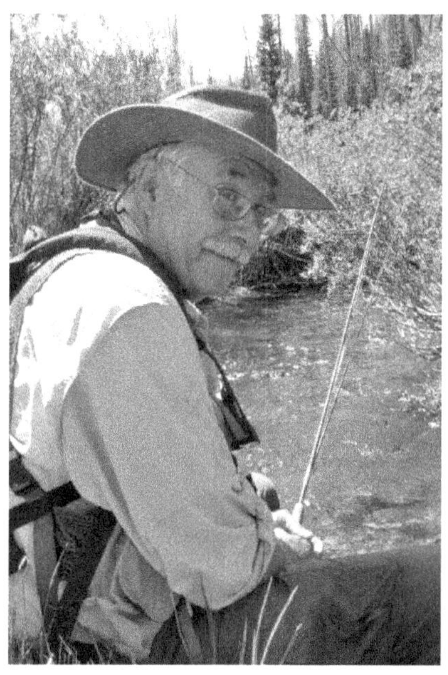

Greg Moore is a 25-year veteran of the Central Intelligence Agency where he spent his government career developing devices and concepts for use in Agency operations. He is a former Chief Scientist of the Agency's research office and a former Editor-in-Chief of *The Journal of Intelligence Community Research and Development*.

Prior to his government career, he held positions as an industrial research scientist with Masonite Corporation in Chicago, Illinois and as an assistant professor at the Virginia Polytechnic Institute and State University in Blacksburg, Virginia.

He holds BS, MS, and PhD degrees from The Pennsylvania State University, University Park, Pennsylvania and a Master of Engineering Science degree from Loyola University, Baltimore, Maryland.

His prior books include: *Properties and Processing of Polymers for Engineers* (with D.E. Kline), and *Failing Forward Fast: What 25 Years in the CIA Taught Us about Getting Things Done in Bureaucracies* (first and second editions with B.M. Hartmann).

End Notes

[1] This phrasing is taken from a well-known saying that "A great many people think they are thinking when they are merely rearranging their prejudices." The saying is most popularly attributed to the 19th century philosopher, William James. While James' writing suggested similar ideas, he did not use these exact words. The exact wording is more likely that of William Fitzjames Oldham. It is a simple example of how the internet and other media can popularize something that is not quite true. See, for example,
https://quoteinvestigator.com/2017/05/10/merely/

[2] Kahneman, D., *Thinking, Fast and Slow*, Farrar, Straus, and Giroux, New York, 2011, p. 98.

[3] Clearly, System 2 can also be biased and prone to mistakes.

[4] *Wikipedia*, "The Muller-Lyer Illusion,"
https://en.wikipedia.org/wiki/M%C3%BCller-Lyer_illusion

[5] These three questions are known as the Cognitive Reflection Test. See, for example, Frederick, S., "Cognitive Reflection and Decision Making," *The Journal of Economic Perspectives*, Vol. 19, No. 4 (Autumn, 2005), pp. 25-42.

[6] For an excellent review of our unconscious thinking, see Cal Tech theoretical physicist Leonard Mlodinow's book, *Subliminal How Your Unconscious Mind Rules Your Behavior*, Vintage Books, New York, 2013. On page 5 he notes: "we all possess a rich and active unconscious life that plays out in parallel to our conscious thoughts and feelings and has a powerful effect on them, in ways we are only now beginning to be able to measure with some degree of accuracy."

[7] Some parts of this chapter and the one that follows are adapted from an earlier book, *Failing Forward Fast Second Edition: What 25 Years in the CIA Taught Us About Getting Things Done in Bureaucracies*, KJI Ltd, Pueblo. 2018. *Failing Forward Fast* is about solving technical problems related to espionage, a topic for which deliberation is absolutely critical.

[8] McGurk, H. and J. MacDonald, "Hearing Lips and Seeing Voices," *Nature* 264, (December 23, 1976): pp. 746 - 748.

[9] For example, see Medina, J.," McGurk Effect (with explanation)"

---

https://www.youtube.com/watch?v=jtsfidRq2tw

[10] Simons, D. and C. Chabris, "Gorillas in Our Midst: Sustained Inattentional Blindness for Dynamic Events," *Perception,* 1999, 28 (9): pp. 1059 - 1074.

[11] Some of my favorites that are easy reads include: *You are Not So Smart* by David McRaney; *Why We Make Mistakes* by Joseph Hallinan; The *Invisible Gorilla by* Christopher Chabris and Daniel Simons; and *Predictably Irrational* by Dan Ariely.

[12] Twain, M., and Cardwell, G. (ed.), *The Innocents Abroad or The New Pilgrims' Progress,* American Publishing Company, Hartford, 1869, p.381. https://www.gutenberg.org/files/3176/3176-h/3176-h.htm

[13] McRaney, D., *You are Not So Smart,* New York: Penguin Group, 2011), pp. 214-219.

[14] The placebo effect refers to improvement occurring because of a patient's belief in the cure rather than any biological effect of the treatment. The opposite of the placebo effect is the nocebo effect, in which patients exhibit negative symptoms when treated with an inert substance that they believe is harmful.

[15] Singh, S., "Did we really witness the 'amazing power' of acupuncture?" *The Telegraph*, 14 Feb 2006.
https://www.telegraph.co.uk/news/science/science-news/3344833/Did-we-really-witness-the-amazing-power-of-acupuncture.html

[16] This is in no way meant to minimize the significance of the real problems that many U.S. residents face today.

[17] For perspective: as of October 2018, there were 2,401 U.S. military deaths in Afghanistan and 4,550 military deaths in the Iraq. See, for example, Crawford, C., "Human Cost of the Post-9/11 Wars: Lethality and the Need for Transparency," November 2018.
https://watson.brown.edu/costsofwar/files/cow/imce/papers/2018/Human%20Costs%2C%20Nov%208%202018%20CoW.pdf
and *Veteran's Administration web site,* "America's Wars Fact Sheet,"
https://www.va.gov/opa/publications/factsheets/fs_americas_wars.pdf

[18] Mackay, C., *Extraordinary Popular Delusions and the Madness of Crowds*, Richard Bentley, London, 1841.

---

[19] *Pets.com* was one of the more visible failures of the dot-com era. It was a pet food and supplies company built on an unsustainable business model.

[20] This is usually referred to as an *ad hominem* argument.

[21] This is known as an argument from authority, or *argumentum ab auctoritate.*

[22] A recent example is the frenzy over cannabidiol (CBD), a compound obtained from either hemp or marijuana plants. While CBD does have some medicinal benefits (for example, reducing seizures in some forms of epilepsy), some of the claims being made by vendors are completely unproven.

[23] This is known as the *post-hoc, ergo propter hoc* argument.

[24] There are a number of references that deal with logical fallacies in great detail. See, for example, Bennett, B., *Logically Fallacious: The Ultimate Collection of Over 300 Logical Fallacies)*, Archieboy, Sudbury, 2018. https://www.amazon.com/dp/1456624539/ref=rdr_ext_tmb

[25] The "^" symbol means "to the power of."

[26] Currently, computational neuroscientists do not know how much data is stored in a synapse. The number could be greater or less than one.

[27] The calculation assumes that streaming standard definition television requires about 1 GB per hour.

[28] Loftus, E, "The Fiction of Memory," TED Talk transcript. https://www.lingq.com/lesson/elizabeth-loftus-the-fiction-of-memory-349322/

[29] Kahneman, D., "The Riddle of Experience," *TED Talk web site.* https://www.ted.com/talks/daniel_kahneman_the_riddle_of_experience_vs_memory?language=en

[30] Feynman, R., "Cargo Cult Science, Some Remarks on Science, Pseudoscience, and Learning How to Not Fool Yourself," Caltech Address, 1974, *California Institute of Technology website.* http://calteches.library.caltech.edu/51/2/CargoCult.htm

[31] If Einstein's equation doesn't work for you, try these other examples from everyday life: the weather (why do high and low pressure zones

---

rotate in different directions?); computers (what are blockchains and bitcoins?); and common machinery (how does a sewing machine work?).

[32].Kruger, J., and D. Dunning, "Unskilled and Unaware of It: How Difficulties in Recognizing One's Own Incompetence Lead to Inflated Self-assessments," *J Pers Soc Psychol.* 1999 Dec;77(6), pp. 1121-34. Also, Dunning, D., "The Dunning–Kruger Effect," *Advances in Experimental Social Psychology*, 44, December 2011, pp. 247-296. The term "metacognition" is the ability to stand back and assess our own thinking.

32

[33] Cross, K.P., "Not Can, But Will College Teaching be Improved?", *New Directions for Higher Education*, Volume 1977, Issue17, Spring 1977, pp. 1-15. https://onlinelibrary.wiley.com/doi/abs/10.1002/he.36919771703

[34] The actual criteria as listed on the *Darwin Awards web site* are: (1) reproduction: out of the gene pool, either dead or sterile; (2) excellence: astounding misapplication of judgment; (3) self-selection: cause one's own demise; (4) maturity: capable of sound judgment; and (5) veracity: the event must be true.

[35] If this is confusing, try an experiment using rubber bands instead of thinking about coiled springs. Cut three pieces from a rubber band, two that are identical in length and one that is twice as long. Hold the two short pieces together and pull on them. Now pull on the larger piece with about the same force. The amount of extension in the long piece will be about four times that in the short pieces.

[36] For a mathematical treatment of this and related counterintuitive systems, see Cohen, J.E., and P. Horowitz, "Paradoxical Behavior of Mechanical and Electrical Networks," *Nature*, Vol 352, (22 Aug 1991), pp. 699-701.

[37] Sinclair, U., *The Jungle*, Penguin, New York, 1960. See also, Ariely, D., *Predictably Irrational The Hidden Forces That Shape Our Decisions*, Harper Collins, New York, 2008, pp. 226-227. Another term for this effect is "motivated reasoning."

[38] Some are better than others. *Charity Watch*, for example, rates charities from A to F based upon how much of their donations go to programs and how much the charity spends to raise $100. Similarly, *BBB Watch* only approves charities that spend no more than 35% of their donations on administrative costs https://www.consumerreports.org/charities/best-charities-for-your-donations/

[39] See, for example, Dickey, C., "Grand Old Paranoia: How Republican conspiracy theories have warped Washington," *The New Republic web site*, November 14, 2018. https://newrepublic.com/article/152195/grand-old-paranoia-republican-conspiracy-theories-warp-washington

[40] Lyme disease is a bacterial infection carried by deer ticks. Genomic evidence shows that the bacterium that causes the disease has existed in North America for tens of thousands of years, far longer than the U.S. Department of Defense. See, for example, "Ancient History of Lyme Disease in North America Revealed with Bacterial Genomes," Yale School of Public Health, August 28, 2017. https://publichealth.yale.edu/news-article/15651/

[41] You just might be saying: sure, most of those are bogus, but this one .....

[42] Some of these are from *Rational Wikipedia*, "List of Conspiracy Theories," https://rationalwiki.org/wiki/List_of_conspiracy_theories#Economic_and_business_conspiracy_theories

[43] Oliver, J.E., and T. J. Wood, "Conspiracy Theories and the Paranoid Style(s) of Mass Opinion," *American Journal of Political Science*, Vol. 58, No. 4, October 2014, pp. 952–966

[44] *Merriam Webster Online Dictionary*, "Conspiracy Theory," https://www.merriam-webster.com/dictionary/conspiracy%20theory

[45] Jolley, D., and K.M. Douglas, "The Effects of Anti-Vaccine Conspiracy Theories on Vaccination Intentions," *PLoS One*. 2014; 9(2): e89177.

[46] Shermer, M., "The Conspiracy Theory Detector," *Scientific American web site*, December 1, 2010. https://www.scientificamerican.com/article/the-conspiracy-theory-director/

[47] Wood, C., "Santa Fe Institute," COFES 2012, Congress on the Future of Engineering Software. https://www.youtube.com/wtch?v=UYBT13Znq2k

[48] Henig, R., "Looking for the Lie," *The New York Times web site*, 5 February 2006. https://www.nytimes.com/2006/02/05/magazine/looking-for-the-lie.html

[49] "Research Methods in Psychology," *Study.com website*

---

https://study.com/academy/lesson/deception-definition-meaning-quiz.html

50 We usually think in terms of five basic senses: hearing, sight, smell, taste, and touch. There are, however, at least two more, vestibular and proprioception, that deal with position and movement of the body in space. They allow us, for example, to walk without watching our feet all of the time. If you have ever tried to walk up a set of stairs whose step heights vary, you understand how easy it is to fool these other systems.

51 Gabor, T., *Everybody does it!: Crime by the Public*, University of Toronto Press, Toronto, 1994, p. 58.

52 Rhode, D.L., *Cheating: Ethics in Everyday Life*, Oxford University Press, Oxford, 2018, Chapter 1.

53 Sherman, M., "Why We Don't Give Each Other a Break," *Psychology Today web site*, June 20, 2014, https://www.psychologytoday.com/us/blog/real-men-dont-write-blogs/201406/why-we-dont-give-each-other-break

54 The IRS estimates that Americans now cheat the government to the tune of about $½ trillion per year. The IRS collects about $3 ½ trillion per year, so the cheating rate is about 12%. http://www.thefiscaltimes.com/2016/04/29/IRS-Now-Pegs-Tax-Cheating-Americans-458-Billion-Annually

55 Rhode, D.L., *Cheating: Ethics in Everyday Life*, Oxford University Press, Oxford, 2018, p.3.

56 Some of these examples are clearly unethical, but I am not suggesting that all of them are. I am only suggesting that we should understand the methods and try to make our decisions based somewhat on merit, not just the particular heart strings that they are pulling.

57 Charles Revson founded Revlon along with Joseph Revson and Charles Lachman in 1932. https://www.brainyquote.com/authors/charles_revson

58 Underhill, P., *Why We Buy: The Science of Shopping*, Simon and Schuster, New York, 2009 and Alter, A., *Irresistible The Rise of Addictive Technology and the Business of Keeping Us Hooked*, Penguin, New York, 2017.

59 The "con" in con man refers to "confidence."

---

[60] "Dark pattern" is a term used for elements of web design that coerce us into doing things that we did not intend to do, such as committing to a long-term subscription when signing up for a free trial. See, for example, https://www.darkpatterns.org/

[61] The Tor browser is a product of the Tor Project, Inc., a non-profit whose mission is to: "advance human rights and defend your privacy online through free software and open networks." *Tor Project web site.* https://www.torproject.org/

[62] Congress can grant jurisdiction authority with the consent of the country in question.

[63] A typical lottery scam employs an email saying that you have won a prize, and requests that you provide a fee and/or information in order to claim it.

[64] In Marc Goodman's book, *Future Crimes, Inside the Digital Underground and the Battle for Our Connected World,* Anchor, New York, 2016, he describes the acronym UPDATE for thinking about cyber protection. (U)date programs frequently; (P)asswords should be long, heterogeneous, and unique; (D)ownload software only from official sites; (A)dministrator accounts should not be used as day-to-day accounts; (T)urn off your computer when you are not using it; (E)ncrypt data that matters.

[65] U.S. Department of Justice, Federal Bureau of Investigation, "Elicitation," *FBI website.* https://www.fbi.gov/file-repository/elicitation-brochure.pdf/view

[66] Nolan, J., *Confidential: Uncover Your Competitors' Top Business Secrets Legally and Quickly--and Protect Your Own,* Harper, New York, 1999.

[67] I have focused on elicitation from a defensive position because the chapter deals with how we can be deceived by others. Clearly, however, good elicitation skills can help make better decisions by drawing out information that is needed. A doctor, lawyer, or engineer can benefit greatly from this skill.

[68] James, W., *The Principles of Psychology, Vol.1.*, Cosimo, New York, 2007. William James is sometimes known as the father of American psychology.

---

[69] If books are not yet available on a subject, pick sources that have the most time between the event and publication. Time is a great filter for errors and hype.

[70]Blinkist is a subscription service that provides summaries of non-fiction titles that can be read or listened to in 10 or 20 minutes. https://www.blinkist.com/

[71] While we really might want to believe that rhinoceros horn powder cured someone's malady, anecdote is generally a poor reason for doing anything serious. There can be many reasons why a particular medical condition turned out as it did. For example, many things tend to get better over time on their own (an effect called regression to the mean). Similarly, the placebo effect can make people feel better subjectively without addressing the real problem. And, finally, the anecdote process tends to filter out the cases where the treatment did not work. Someone who took the powder and later died won't have much to say about the matter.

[72] As we will see later on, even good journals get things wrong and should be considered cautiously. That is the nature of science. The solution is not, however, to surround ourselves instead with fringe material that sometimes populates weak journals.

[73] Stewart, D., "My Great-Great-Grandfather Hated the Gettysburg Address. 150 Years Later, He's Famous For It," *Smithsonian Magazine web site*, November 18, 2013, https://www.smithsonianmag.com/history/my-great-great-grandfather-hated-the-gettysburg-address-150-years-later-hes-famous-for-it-180947746/

[74] Casey, W., "How to Read a Book," in the Inventory of the William J. Casey Papers at the *Online Archive of California web site.* https://oac.cdlib.org/findaid/ark:/13030/kt1s20357r/entire_text/

[75] While I could clearly do this on a computer, there is something about wandering a bookstore and touching the books that makes for a better experience. This could simply be a remnant of an early life spent wandering library stacks.

[76] Mark Strauss, "Ten Inventions Inspired by Science Fiction," *Smithsonian web site.* http://www.smithsonianmag.com/science-nature/ten-inventions-inspired-by-science-fiction-128080674/

[77] Moore, G., *The Last Days of Night*, Random House, New York, 2016.

---

[78] For an interesting expose of how junky web media can get, see Holliday, R., *Trust Me, I'm Lying, Confessions of a Media Manipulator*, Portfolio/Penguin, New York, 2017.

[79] Nutritionists are far less regulated than dieticians and most doctors know relatively little about nutrition and health.

[80] The term *consensus* is perhaps a bit misleading. As used here, it does not mean something that everyone agrees on, but rather represents a belief that is held by most scientists or practitioners at the time. There are many cases where the consensus has turned out to be false, and this occurs when new insights emerge. For example, bloodletting was once a very common medical treatment for many ailments. It is now considered valid only for a rare condition involving the buildup of iron in the blood.

[81] While some of the deep web's content is sketchy (the "dark web" that is used for anonymous criminal activities such as markets for our stolen credit cards), most of it is business archives, fee-based services, personal accounts, and other password protected sites. We can see how this works with a simple experiment. If we google our own name, none of our bank account statements show up. Yet we can type in the proper URL and password and view these data on our computer.

[82] The term is a play on the term "AstroTurf ®" as a fake grass. See, for example, *Wikipedia*, "Astroturfing,"
https://en.wikipedia.org/wiki/Astroturfing

[83] Robert Hanssen was an FBI agent who spied for the Russians from 1979 to 2001. Aldrich Ames was a CIA case officer who spied for the Russians from 1985 to 1994. Of course, these cautions also apply to retail products, charitable appeals, financial offers, medical advice, and all other products of the virtual marketplace.

[84] This is a time-tested strategy used by intelligence analysts. While an adversary might be able to distort one channel of information (say, for example, by dangling a human source to convey a certain impression), it is hard to distort all channels of information so that they all convey the same message. As a result, intelligence analysts look for confirmation or rebuttal of information in other channels, such as by reading the opposition's secure communications. See, for example, Bennett, M., and E. Waltz, *Counterdeception Principles and Applications for National Security*, Artec House, Norwood, MA, 2007, p.247.

[85] Hans Rosling passed away in 2017. His son and daughter-in-law now carry on the work.
https://www.gapminder.org/

---

86 Rosling, H., O. Rosling, and A.R. Rönnlund, *Factfulness: Ten Reasons We're Wrong About the World – and Why Things Are Better Than You Think*, Flatiron Books, New York, 2018.

87 Zhang, M., "The First Hoax Photograph Ever Shot," *PetaPixel web site*, November 15, 2012, https://petapixel.com/2012/11/15/the-first-hoax-photograph-ever-shot/

88 Harwell, D., "Faked Pelosi videos, slowed to make her appear drunk, spread across social media," *Washington Post web site,* May 23, 2019. https://www.washingtonpost.com/technology/2019/05/23/faked-pelosi-videos-slowed-make-her-appear-drunk-spread-across-social-media/?utm_term=.5d92ebdfb2bd

89 Mak, T., "Technologies to Create Fake Audio and Video are Quickly Evolving," *National Public Radio web site*, April 2, 2018, https://www.npr.org/2018/04/02/598916380/technologies-to-create-fake-audio-and-video-are-quickly-evolving

90 This is not meant to imply that we should completely ignore other sources of information that contradict the mainstream. There are often new options to consider. But we should also be cautious with anything or anyone that disagrees with information that we have found to be reliable in the past.

91 Always keep in mind that experts are sometimes wrong. Doctors misdiagnose patients. Scientists publish work that is later debunked. Stock brokers can barely make the average. See, for example, Freedman, D.H., *Wrong Why Experts Keep Failing Us — And How to Know When Not to Trust Them*, Little, Brown and Company, New York, 2010, pp.231-236. Also, Kahneman, D., *Thinking Fast and Slow*, Farrar, Straus and Giroux, New York, 2011, pp. 234-244.

92 Think of this process as a Socratic method of teaching that involves questioning thought rather than pummeling someone with facts. See, for example, *Socratic Teaching*, in *The Foundation for Critical Thinking web site.*
https://www.criticalthinking.org/pages/socratic-teaching/606

93 Moore, G. and B. Hartmann, *Failing Forward Fast 2nd Ed. What 25 Years in the CIA Taught Us about Getting Things Done in Bureaucracies*, KJI Ltd, Pueblo, 2018, pp. 37-40.

---

[94] See, for example, Ehrenreich, B., *Natural Causes: An Epidemic of Wellness, the Certainty of Dying, and Killing Ourselves to Live Longer*, Hatchet, New York, 2018.

[95] Frizell, S., "Nearly One in Ten Americans Think Vaccines Are Unsafe," *Time Magazine web site*, February 9, 2015, http://time.com/3701543/measles-vaccines-poll-anti-vaxxers/

[96] While the emphasis in this chapter is on science, some aspects of engineering research create similar levels of confusion and uncertainty.

[97] Collins, H. and T. Pinch, *The Golem, What Everyone Should Know about Science*, Cambridge University Press, Cambridge, 1991, pp. 150-151. A golem is a mythical creature made of clay and water. While often characterized as a servant, its activities can sometimes go awry and wreak havoc.

[98] NASA, "Mars Climate Orbiter Team Finds Likely Cause of Loss, Release," National Aeronautics and Space Administration, Release 99-113, *NASA web site*, September 30, 1999, https://mars.nasa.gov/msp98/news/mco990930.html

[99] While peer review usually occurs once a paper is drafted, it can occur at any time in the process. Proposals for research are typically peer reviewed by funding organizations like the National Science Foundation. In some fields, experimental procedures are submitted to journals for review before the work is done.

[100] Carpi, A., A.E. Egger, and N.H. Kuldell, "Peer Review in Scientific Publishing," *VisonLearning web site*, https://www.visionlearning.com/en/library/Process-of-Science/49/Peer-Review-in-Scientific-Publishing/159

[101] See, for example, *Public Library of Science web site*, https://www.plos.org/

[102] Baker, M., "1,500 Scientists Lift the Lid on Reproducibility," *Nature web site*, 533, 25 May 2016. https://www.nature.com/news/1-500-scientists-lift-the-lid-on-reproducibility-1.19970

[103] The example is an extreme case simply to illustrate the general idea behind dominance of false positives. Scientists can reduce this false positive bias by careful selection of potentially meaningful relationships to study, and publication of negative, as well as positive, results. The example

was taken from Ioannides, J.P.A., "Why Most Published Research Findings Are False," *PLOS Med*, August 30, 2005, vol. 2, issue 8. https://journals.plos.org/plosmedicine/article?id=10.1371/journal.pmed.0020124

[104]Another bias in positive reporting lies in the retraction process. Retractions never get the publicity that the original media show provided. Many are surprised, for example, that the original scientific research linking autism to vaccine was retracted, and its author lost his medical license. Of course, there are also conspiracy theorists who say the author's medical license was pulled to keep the status quo.

[105] Feynman, R., "Cargo Cult Science," 1974 Caltech Commencement address, *California Institute of Technology web site* http://calteches.library.caltech.edu/51/2/CargoCult.htm

[106] See, for example, Samuel Arbesman's *The Half-Life of Facts: Why Everything We Know Has an Expiration Date*, Penguin, New York, 2013.

[107] Asimov, I., *The Relativity of Wrong*, Doubleday, New York, 1988, pp. 213-225.

[108] "Who's fat? New definition adopted," *CNN web site*, June 17, 1998, http://www.cnn.com/HEALTH/9806/17/weight.guidelines/

[109] Offit, P.A., *Pandora's Lab: Seven Stories of Science Gone Wrong*, National Geographic, Washington, DC, 2017, pp.41-59.

[110] Our understanding is still far from complete.

[111] This decline resulted largely from public health and sanitation improvements such as the availability of clean drinking water.

[112] "Leading Causes of Death, *1900-1998," United States Center for Disease Control web site.* https://www.cdc.gov/nchs/data/dvs/lead1900_98.pdf

[113] Forouhi, N.G., R. M. Krauss, G. Taubes, and W. Willett, "Dietary Fat and Cardiometabolic Health: Evidence, Controversies, and Consensus for Guidance," *The BMJ web site*, 2018: 361, 13 June, 2018. https://www.bmj.com/content/361/bmj.k2139

[114] Mozaffarian, D., "Dietary and Policy Priorities for Cardiovascular Disease, Diabetes, and Obesity: A Comprehensive Review," *Circulation*, 2016 Jan 12;133(2):187-225. https://www.ncbi.nlm.nih.gov/pubmed/26746178

---

[115] Arrhenius, S., "On the Influence of Carbonic Acid in the Air upon the Temperature of the Ground," *Philosophical Magazine and Journal of Science*, Series 4, Vol. 41, April 1896, pp. 237-276. https://www.rsc.org/images/Arrhenius1896_tcm18-173546.pdf

[116] Of course, there are still scientists who disagree with this general conclusion. As more work is done, their objections will either lead to changes in the consensus, or they will be rejected.

[117] N. Oreskes, and E. Conway, *Merchants of Doubt: How a Handful of Scientists Obscured the Truth on Issues from Tobacco Smoke to Global Warming,* Bloomsbury Press, New York, 2010.

[118] Gustafson, A., and M. Goldberg, "Even Americans highly concerned about climate change dramatically underestimate the scientific consensus," *Yale Program on Climate Change web site,* Oct 18, 2018. https://climatecommunication.yale.edu/publications/even-americans-highly-concerned-about-climate-change-dramatically-underestimate-the-scientific-consensus/

[119] Hoofnagle, M., "Climate change deniers: failsafe tips on how to spot them," March 11, 2009, *Guardian web site.* https://www.theguardian.com/environment/blog/2009/mar/10/climate-change-denier

[120] In other applications, simply knowing that a relationship exists is sufficient. For example, insurance companies use credit reports to help determine risk without completely understanding why the two factors are correlated. See, for example, Mayer-Schönberger, V., and K. Cukier, *Big Data*, Houghton Mifflin Harcourt, Boston, 2014

[121] This example is adapted from Reinhart, A., *Statistics Done Wrong*, No Starch Press, San Francisco, 2015, pp. 16-18.

[122] Low power will also tend to cause erroneous positive results. See, for example, Button, K.S., J.P.A Ioannidis, C. Mokrysz, B. A. Nosek, J. Flint, E. S. J. Robinson, and M. R. Munafò, "Power failure: why small sample size undermines the reliability of neuroscience," *Nature Reviews Neuroscience,* vol 14, May 2013, pp. 365-376. https://brain.mpg.de/fileadmin/user_upload/images/IMPRS/Master_Reading_List/small_samples_Nature_Reviews.pdf

[123] According to those who use optimality models: "Current incentive structures are in conflict with maximizing the scientific value of research," See A.D. Higginson and M.R. Munafo, "Current Incentives for

---

Scientists Lead to Underpowered Studies with Erroneous Conclusions," PLoS Biology November 2016;14(11).
https://journals.plos.org/plosbiology/article?id=10.1371/journal.pbio.2000995

[124] Meta-analyses are used in a variety of research fields including medicine, psychology and education. But its first application was astronomy. See, for example, O'Rourke, K., "A historical perspective on meta-analysis: dealing quantitatively with varying study results," *JLL Bulletin: Commentaries on the history of treatment evaluation*, 2006
https://www.jameslindlibrary.org/articles/a-historical-perspective-on-meta-analysis-dealing-quantitatively-with-varying-study-results/

[125] As noted earlier, a journal's impact factor is a measure of the number of citations that articles in the journal receive. See "*Journal impact measures*," University of Minnesota Libraries, Minneapolis, MN.
https://www.lib.umn.edu/researchsupport/impact/journals#jif

[126] See, for example, "How Do You Know a Journal is Legitimate?," Stoney Brook University Libraries.
http://www.library.stonybrook.edu/scholarly-communication/know-journal-legitimate/
See also, Laine, C., and M.A. Winker, "Identifying predatory or pseudo-journals," *Biochem Med (Zagreb)*. 2017 Jun 15; 27(2): 285–291.
https://www.ncbi.nlm.nih.gov/pmc/articles/PMC5493175/

[127] Perhaps the most famous example of taking scientific results public before subjecting the results to peer review was Martin Fleishman and Stanley Pons' public announcement of the discovery of cold fusion in 1989. Both were chemists at the University of Utah who thought they had discovered a way to create nuclear fusion at room temperature. While some research into cold fusion continues today, their specific experiments were quickly debunked by other scientists.

[128] Most clinical drug trials, for example, are funded by industry rather than the government. The government only funds about 15% of clinical trials, but these can often be the most useful for consumers. For example, a clinical trial by a drug company might compare a drug to a placebo while a federally-funded trial might compare the drug to other drugs that have similar purposes. As a consumer, you would like to know which of the drugs is the better value. See Cohn, M., "Industry Funds Six Times More Clinical Trials than Feds, Research Shows," *The Baltimore Sun web site*, December 15, 2015.
https://www.baltimoresun.com/health/bs-hs-trial-funding-20151214-story.html

---

[129] Thill, S., Margaret Atwood, Speculative Fiction's Apocalyptic Optimist, *Wired web site*, October 28, 1989. https://www.wired.com/2009/10/margaret-atwood-speculative-fictions-apocalyptic-optimist/

[130] Paulos, J.A., *Innumeracy: Mathematical Illiteracy and Its Consequences,* Hill and Yang, New York, 2001.

[131] Chu, D., "An Eminent Math Professor Says "innumeracy" Rivals Illiteracy as a Cause for Concern in America," *People.com web site*, May 29, 1989. https://people.com/archive/an-eminent-math-professor-says-innumeracy-rivals-illiteracy-as-a-cause-for-concern-in-america-vol-31-no-21/

[132] I don't intend to demean calculus or geometry. The thought processes that they teach are valuable, even if the specific results might not be at the moment.

[133] Grossman, L., "Only a small fraction of space has been searched for aliens," *Science News for Students web site*, October 24, 2018 https://www.sciencenewsforstudents.org/

[134] Here are a few more. If fear of sharks is our problem, the number of U.S. deaths caused by sharks each year is about 20 times less than the number of deaths from cows. If we are thinking of retiring, that $300,000 nest egg we've saved for retirement might be equivalent to only 10 years at our current lifestyle. If we are watching salt consumption for health reasons, the 1380 grams of sodium in a can of Progresso Chicken Noodle soup is 92% of the total amount we should consume in a day.

[135] Heuristics aren't limited to mathematics, of course. The familiar *i before e except after c* is an example of a spelling heuristic.

[136] A logarithm is nothing more than an exponent referenced to a particular base (like 10). The number 72, for example, can be expressed as 10 raised to the 1.8573 power, where 1.8573 is the logarithm of 72. The biggest hurdle is perhaps getting past the common misimpression that an exponent is always a whole number like 2 or 3. You can raise a number to any power you like. The Khan Academy web site is a good place to start to learn about logarithms. https://www.khanacademy.org

[137] To solve an equation containing an exponent, take the logarithm of both sides, where Log A^B = B Log A.

---

138 Einstein is sometimes credited with saying that compound interest is the eighth wonder of the world. He who understands it, earns it. He who doesn't pays it.

139 Rettner, R., "The Weight of the World: Researchers Weigh Human Population," *Live Science web site*, June 17, 2012, https://www.livescience.com/36470-human-population-weight.html

140 The term "exponential" has become to some extent synonymous with increasing rapidly and nonlinearly. But not everything that increases rapidly and nonlinearly is (technically) exponential. There is, for example, a difference between y=x^n (rapid and nonlinear, but not exponential growth) and y=n^x (exponential growth) when x and y are variables and n is a constant. In any case, it is the surprising rapidity with which change can occur that makes decision making (or putting off decisions) risky.

141 Traganidas, G., "Quotes Charlie Munger," *Berkshire Hathaway: The Practical Way*, December 20, 2010. http://www.thepracticalway.com/2010/12/20/quotes-charlie-munger/

142 NOAA National Centers for Environmental Information, NOAA Climate at a Glance, *National Oceanic and Atmospheric Association web site.* https://www.ncdc.noaa.gov/cag/national/mapping/

143 Cherry picking is the idea that you pick only the most desirable examples of something. The term likely comes from the idea of rummaging through a bowl of cherries, picking out the best ones to eat.

144 Some other pitfalls of graphs and charts include: using pie charts when the data do not sum to 100%, not clearly labeling axes, abusing three dimensional effects to exaggerate differences, and not following conventions (the graph is drawn upside down, for example).

145 Cairo, A., *How Charts Lie: Getting Smarter about Visual Information*, W. W. Norton, New York, 2019.

146 One of the difficulties in comparing risk and benefit is that costs are often externalized. When a company produces a product, some of the cost of that production is borne by society rather than the company and its stockholders. Some examples include: water pollution, noise, climate change, increased crime, etc.

147 This in no way is meant to disregard proven consequences of low levels of certain contaminants on our health. Some things are really nasty at very low levels.

[148] "Vehicle Deaths Estimated at 40,000 for Third Straight Year," *National Safety Council web site.* https://www.nsc.org/road-safety/safety-topics/fatality-estimates

[149] "Sports Injury Statistics," *Stanford Children's Health web site.* https://www.stanfordchildrens.org/en/topic/default?id=sports-injury-statistics-90-P02787

[150] Abassi, L., "Alcohol the Most Dangerous Drug in the World," *American Council on Science and Health web site,* December 23, 2015, https://www.acsh.org/news/2015/12/23/alcohol-the-most-dangerous-drug-in-the-world

[151] Offit, P., *The Cutter Incident How America's First Polio Vaccine Led to the Growing Vaccine Crisis,* Yale University Press, New Haven and London, 2005. These numbers (especially the number who fell ill) vary somewhat in the literature.

[152] Beaubien, J., "Wiping Out Polio: How the U.S. Snuffed Out A Killer," *National Public Radio web site,* October 15, 2012. https://www.npr.org/sections/health-shots/2012/10/16/162670836/wiping-out-polio-how-the-u-s-snuffed-out-a-killer

[153] There are many "me versus us" problems in the modern world. For example, work on the Yucca Mountain (Nevada) began in 1980s as the nation's underground nuclear waste repository. It is still in limbo due to local protests, despite the high risks to all that are associated with storing nearly 90,000 tons of nuclear waste in temporary facilities across the United States.

[154] Of course, if you are the one unlucky soul who defies the odds, then it is not inconsequential to you.

[155] Based on data from 1990 through 2003. See, for example, "Lightning Fatalities, Injuries, and Damage Reports in the United States," *National Lightning Safety Institute web site.* http://lightningsafety.com/nlsi_lls/fatalities_us.html

[156] A population is simply a group. It might be the people who reside in a particular country or state, a particular species of animal, the students in a classroom, or even the remaining 1957 Chevrolets in the U.S.

[157] Most of us think in terms of two types of averages: the arithmetic mean and the median. Occasionally, someone will toss in the mode, which is

---

simply the most frequent value in a series of numbers. But there are others. For example, the geometric mean multiplies all of the n values together and then takes the nth root. It can be a useful tool for a series of positive numbers that are skewed. See, for example, "Geometric Mean: Definition, Examples, Formula, Uses," *Statistics How To web site.* https://www.statisticshowto.datasciencecentral.com/geometric-mean-2/

158 Mahoney C.R., G.E. Giles, B.P. Marriott, D.A. Judelson, E.L. Glickman, P.J. Geiselman, and H.R. Lieberman, "Intake of caffeine from all sources and reasons for use by college students," *Clinical Nutrition*, 2019 Apr;38(2), pp. 668-675. *National Library of Medicine, National Institutes of Health PubMed web site.* https://www.ncbi.nlm.nih.gov/pubmed/29680166

159 When you see an average that supposedly represents the population, ask what the margin of error is. In the coffee example, if the reported average was 4 cups per day, its significance would vary depending on whether the margin of error was ½ cup per day (the real number is between 3 ½ and 4 ½) or 3 cups per day. (the real number is between 1 cup per day and 7 cups per day). In such cases, it is often better to think in terms of a range than a single average number.

160 The calculation is often done using Bayes Theorem. This theorem is based on the idea of conditional probabilities, or the probability that something is true, given something else is true. See, for example, https://www.youtube.com/watch?v=i7OY7CZUdIY

161 If you are still not convinced, simply run through all of the possibilities for the two cases of the original problem where you pick the first door and (1) it contains the car, and (2) it doesn't. If you stay with the original pick, you will win one time out of three. If you switch, you will win two times out of three.

162 "High School Statistics: Probability," *Khan Academy Website,* https://www.khanacademy.org/math/probability/probability-geometry

163 The odds of winning the grand prize in Powerball are about 1 in 300,000,000. Between the ages of 18 and 90, there are 3,796 weeks, or twice that number of games. Your chances of winning are the number of times you play divided by the number of possible combinations of numbers (300,000,000) that can be drawn, or about 1 in 39,000.

164 For perspective, 19,000 lottery tickets would weigh on the order of 40 pounds. Over a lifetime, the weight would exceed 150 tons.

---

[165] Unfortunately, studies show that those who can least afford to play the lottery are the dominant customers. A recent study by Bankrate (a consumer financial services company) found that "Households with incomes of $75,000 and above spent $105 a year on lottery tickets, a quarter of what low-income homes spent." See, for example, Gibson, K., "Who buys lottery tickets? Those who can least afford them," *CBS News Moneywatch web site*, September 12, 2018. https://www.cbsnews.com/news/who-buys-lottery-tickets-those-who-can-least-afford-them/

[166] You can increase your odds of not having to share a pot with others by simply avoiding common numbers like birthdays (numbers up to 31).

[167] This excerpt is taken in part from an earlier book, *Failing Forward Fast, 2nd Edition What 25 Years in the CIA Taught Us about Getting Things Done in Bureaucracies*, that I co-authored with Bruce Hartmann, KJI Ltd, Pueblo, Colorado, 2018, pp. 56-62.

[168] Cologuard clinical study results as reported in the Cologuard Patient Guide, p. 33. https://www.accessdata.fda.gov/cdrh_docs/pdf13/P130017c.pdf

[169] The test doesn't do as well detecting precancerous conditions, only finding them about 42% of the time. I've ignored this detail in the calculations.

[170] Incidence is defined medically as the rate of occurrence of new cases of a disease. The rate used here is taken from Siegel, R.L., S.A. Fedewa, W.F. Anderson, K.D. Miller, J. Ma, P.S. Rosenberg, and A. Jemal, "Colorectal Cancer Incidence Patterns in the United States, 1974-2013,". *Journal of the National Cancer Institute*, 109(8) 2017 https://academic.oup.com/jnci/article/109/8/djw322/3053481

[171] The mathematical technique used to make these types of calculation is Bayes Theorem. As noted in an earlier reference, this theorem is based on the idea of conditional probability, or the probability that something is true, given something else is true. In this example, the conditional probability that I calculated was the probability of cancer given a positive test. Note that this is different from the probability of a positive test given that cancer exists.

[172] Adams, D., *The Hitchhiker's Guide to the Galaxy*, Del Rey, New York, 2017, p. 3.

[173] Swartz, C., *Back of the Envelope Physics*, The Johns Hopkins University Press, Baltimore, 2003, and Weinstein, L. and J.A. Adam,

---

Guesstimation: Solving the World's Problems on the Back of a Cocktail Napkin, Princeton University Press, Princeton, New Jersey, 2008.

[174] Cook, M. and R. Clifford, *Mathematicians: An Outer View of the Inner World,* Princeton University Press, 2009, p. 76.

[175] From the television show, *Cheers*, an NBC sitcom involving the activities of the employees and customers of a Boston bar. The comment is from a regular customer, Norm, in response to the bar owner, Sam, asking: "what's happenin' Norm"? The show ran from 1982 to 1993.

[176] Sharkov, D., "Russian City Commissions Statue of Wrong Person in Wikipedia," *Newsweek web site,* August 17, 2018. The *Wikipedia* entry has since been fixed.
https://www.newsweek.com/russian-city-commissions-statue-wrong-patron-wikipedia-mix-1077808

[177] "Bernard M. Baruch>Quotes," *Goodreads*
https://www.goodreads.com/author/quotes/5768330.Bernard_M_Baruch

[178] The effect is sometimes termed the art of the adjacent possible, a term that originated in biology.

[179] "The Man in the Bar," *Mycoted web site.*
https://www.mycoted.com/The_Man_in_the_Bar

[180] One of the more interesting examples of not being able to let go of a bad idea can be found in the annals of WWII. Project Habbakuk was an effort by the Allies to create a gigantic aircraft carrier made of ice. What started as a simple idea (ice floats, so an ice ship shouldn't sink) quickly reached a level of complexity that became impractical. Yet work continued. See, for example, "Project Habbakuk: Britain's secret attempt to build an ice warship," *CNN* web *site*, April 26, 2018.
https://www.cnn.com/style/article/project-habbakuk-ice-aircraft-carrier/index.html

[181] While other handheld calculators preceded the HP-35, Hewlett-Packard's product was the first scientific calculator. Unlike earlier calculators, it could perform more calculations of interest to scientists and engineers.

[182] Sims, P., *Little Bets, How Breakthrough Ideas Emerge from Small Discoveries*, Simon and Schuster, New York, 2011, p. 21.

---

[183] Shariatmadar, D., "Daniel Kahneman: 'What would I eliminate if I had a magic wand? Overconfidence," *The Guardian web site.* https://www.theguardian.com/books/2015/jul/18/daniel-kahneman-books-interview

[184] Lakota elder Joseph M. Marshall III, put it this way: "A truly humble person rarely stumbles because a person walks with his face toward the earth. And, therefore, can see the path ahead. An arrogant person walks with his head held high to bask in the glory of the moment. Such a person is likely to stumble because he or she is more concerned with the moment than what lies ahead." See Marshall, J.M., *Walking with Grandfather The Wisdom of Lakota Elders*, Sounds True, Boulder, 2005, p. 16.

[185] Da Vinci, L., "Of Judging Your Own Picture," Codex Ashburnham, Manuscript 2038, 28 *recto*, in *The Notebooks of Leonardo da Vinci*, Arcturus Publishing Ltd., London, 2017, p. 15. Translations by Edward MacCurdy, p. 15.

[186] Priaulx, W., "Model A Ford Technical Report," *Central Iowa Model A Club* web site, February 2018. http://www.centraliowamodelaclub.com/Model%20A%20Spark%20Advance%20Final.pdf

[187] Consider, for example, how filing income tax forms has changed over the years through the use of products like TurboTax®.

[188] Clifford, C.," Elon Musk: 'Mark my words — A.I. is far more dangerous than nukes,'" *CNBC web site.* https://www.cnbc.com/2018/03/13/elon-musk-at-sxsw-a-i-is-more-dangerous-than-nuclear-weapons.html

[189] Smith, G., *The A.I. Delusion*, Oxford University Press, Oxford, 2018.

[190] Jaques, E., *The Changing Culture of a Factory*, Tavistock, London, 1951.

[191] "International Shark Attack File, Risk of Death," *Florida Museum web site.* https://www.floridamuseum.ufl.edu/shark-attacks/odds/compare-risk/death/

[192] Gill, G., "Availability Cascade," *Cognitive Bias Parade - An Illustrated Review of Misjudgments and Reconstructed Realities web site.* http://www.cognitivebiasparade.com/2014/06/availability-cascade-psychology.html

---

193 Hochma, T., "Decoy Effect: A Complete Practical Guide to The Psychological Pricing and Marketing Hack," *HumanHow web site.* https://humanhow.com/en/the-decoy-effect-complete-guide/

194 Loftus, E. F., "Leading Questions and the Eyewitness Report," *Cognitive Psychology*, 1975, 7, 550-572. http://citeseerx.ist.psu.edu/viewdoc/download?doi=10.1.1.89.2703&rep=rep1&type=pdf

195 "Naïve Realism," *The Human Condition Wiki web site.* http://humancond.org/analysis/mind/naive_realism

196 "List of Cognitive Biases," in *Wikipedia*, https://en.wikipedia.org/wiki/List_of_cognitive_biases
Novella, S., *The Skeptics' Guide to the Universe: How to Know What's Really Real in a World Increasingly Full of Fake*, Grand Central Publishing, New York, 2018.

197 The three major sources for the items in this listing are "List of Fallacies," in *Wikipedia*,
https://en.wikipedia.org/wiki/List_of_fallacies
"Logically Fallacious, The Ultimate Collection of Over 300 Logical Fallacies, Academic Edition," *Logically Fallacious web site*,
https://www.logicallyfallacious.com/tools/lp/Bo/LogicalFallacies
and Novella, S., *The Skeptics' Guide to the Universe: How to Know What's Really Real in a World Increasingly Full of Fake*, Grand Central Publishing, New York, 2018.

198 Taken from "Five Logical Fallacies often used in Political and Policy Debate," *Public Leadership Institute web site*,
https://publicleadershipinstitute.org/2018/08/15/five-logical-fallacies-often-used-political-policy-debate/

199 Much of this section is adapted from the FBI's brochure, "Elicitation," *Federal Bureau of Investigation web site.*
https://www.fbi.gov/file-repository/elicitation-brochure.pdf/view

200 Mitnick, K., *The Art of Deception*, Wiley, Indianapolis, 2002, pp.77-91.

www.ingramcontent.com/pod-product-compliance
Lightning Source LLC
LaVergne TN
LVHW051051080426
835508LV00019B/1822

* 9 7 8 1 7 3 4 3 7 5 1 0 7 *